T5-AFN-038

THE WRITING OF HISTORY

PUBLISHED ON THE FOUNDATION
ESTABLISHED IN MEMORY OF
THEODORE L. GLASGOW

THE WRITING OF HISTORY

AN INTRODUCTION TO HISTORICAL METHOD

BY

FRED MORROW FLING, Ph.D.

PROFESSOR OF EUROPEAN HISTORY IN THE
UNIVERSITY OF NEBRASKA

*"The whole life of man is a perpetual comparison
of evidence and balancing of probabilities."*

NEW HAVEN
YALE UNIVERSITY PRESS
LONDON · HUMPHREY MILFORD · OXFORD UNIVERSITY PRESS
MDCCCCXXVI

ST. IGNATIUS HOUSE OF STUDIES
LIBRARY
MANHASSET

D
16
.F63
1926

COPYRIGHT, 1920, BY
YALE UNIVERSITY PRESS

———

Published, September, 1920
Second printing, August, 1923
Third printing, October, 1926

THE THEODORE L. GLASGOW MEMORIAL
PUBLICATION FUND

The present volume is the second work published by
the Yale University Press on the Theodore L. Glasgow
Memorial Publication Fund.   This Foundation was
established September 17, 1918, by an anonymous gift
to Yale University in memory of Flight Sub-Lieutenant
Theodore L. Glasgow, R.N.   He was born in Montreal,
Canada, May 25, 1898, the eldest son of Robert and
Louise C. Glasgow, and was educated at the University
of Toronto Schools and at the Royal Military College,
Kingston.   In August, 1916, he entered the Royal
Naval Air Service and in July, 1917, went to France
with the Tenth Squadron attached to the Twenty-Second
Wing of the Royal Flying Corps.   A month later, August
19, 1917, he was killed in action on the Ypres front.

TO

ERNST BERNHEIM

Dean of living writers on historical method, whose *Lehrbuch der historischen Methode,* the first detailed and scientific presentation of the process of historical investigation, has been the guide of a generation of scholars, this volume is fittingly dedicated.

FOREWORD

THIS volume is not a revised edition of my *Outline of Historical Method;* it is an entirely new work. It was written for college students who are beginning their studies in historical research, for teachers of history who have had no critical historical training, and for students of history who are hoping to find in private study some compensation for opportunities not enjoyed in college. This book does not aspire to fill the place of Bernheim's *Lehrbuch,* but rather to guide the student through his first steps in research, and to prepare him for the study of Bernheim. In a word, it is an "introduction" to historical method.

Although the simple reading of the text might not, I venture to hope, prove unprofitable, it will, nevertheless, yield the best return when studied in connection with a bit of research exemplifying the process I have endeavored to describe. I would suggest that some limited topic be carefully worked over, all the steps in method being taken from the criticism of the sources to the construction of the final narrative with notes. Only by such an experience can one fully understand what critical historical study means and how difficult and exacting the work of the scientific historian is.

Although this volume does not deal with the teaching of history, it has, nevertheless, an important bearing upon it. A teacher who has not read at least an elementary text on historical method and completed a piece of careful scholarly research, lacks one of the most important parts of the equipment of a well-prepared teacher of history. However much historical information such a teacher may have accumulated, he lacks a scientific standard that would enable him to separate the true from the false, to deal scientifically with contradictory statements in secondary works and to protect himself and his pupils against unsound and superficial historical narratives.

It seems extraordinary that it should be necessary to insist upon the importance of what should be self-evident, but the really extraordinary thing about the pedagogical situation is that a large majority of the teachers of history in secondary schools neither possess an elementary knowledge of historical method nor consider such knowledge a necessary part of their equipment as teachers. A teacher of chemistry who could not direct experimental work in a laboratory could neither secure nor hold a position in a good high school today, but the history courses in the high schools are still "passed around" to teachers without technical training.

Fifteen years ago, in the introduction to my *Outline of Historical Method,* I wrote that "it is the popular belief that any intelligent person, without technical training, can teach a class in history." The statement is almost as true today as it was then, and I am convinced that there will be little improvement in the situation until the technical side of the history teacher's preparation is insisted upon, and he is required to be as much of a professional as the teacher of the natural sciences. Chemistry would be taught in the high schools today by any person who could hold a textbook, had not the practice been rendered impossible by the introduction of laboratory work into the secondary schools, thus making a technically trained teacher a necessity. Why should an acquaintance with the theory and practice of historical method not be required of every high school teacher of history?

The examples in the text have been drawn almost exclusively from the period of the French Revolution. The period is important and interesting enough to justify such a course, but it is probable that I would not have exploited it to quite the same extent had it not been the chosen field for my own researches. I should be glad to attract workers to a field "already white for the harvest." Not only does it offer great opportunities, but for no other period, outside of English or American history, is it so easy to acquire the language equipment which makes possible the reading of the sources in the original text.

The manuscript of my book has been read by Professor George L. Burr, and I have profited by many excellent suggestions touching both matter and form. It is but one of many kindnesses that have marked the long years of our friendship.

It is with a feeling of gratitude that I dedicate this volume to Professor Bernheim. I was groping my way in method at a German university when his *Lehrbuch* appeared; it led me out into the light. It has saved many another lost soul in the quarter of a century of its existence. Bernheim's name should be as familiar to the student of history as Euclid's to the student of mathematics.

FRED MORROW FLING.

CONTENTS

[11]

CONTENTS

The King's Library

I

INTRODUCTION

HISTORICAL method is the process employed in the search for historical truth. But why should we seek for historical truth? How can we justify the expenditure of so much energy by scholars in historical research and the devotion of so much time to historical study in the schools? What benefit do we hope to obtain from it all? Is the entertainment to be found in the observation of the ever changing panorama of the past life of the world the chief cause of our interest in historical study and its sufficient justification? Or is our interest due rather to the import of the content of history, an import so deep for us that the study of history becomes a necessity?

What is history? Unlike Bacon's "jesting Pilate," who asked, "What is truth?" and "would not stay for an answer," the historian must tarry and answer the question he has raised. Turning the pages of a history of the world, we note that it deals with all man's social activities, economic, political, educational, artistic and religious. It describes them, however, not in a state of repose, but of movement and change. In this change, our attention is drawn,

[15]

The King's Library

not to what repeats itself, but to what is new, what has never happened before and can never happen again in the same way. From all this it is evident that the historian is concerned with tracing *the unique evolution of man in his activities as a social being,* the unique life record of humanity. If this be history, then history cannot "repeat itself," there cannot be "historical laws," for a law is a generalization and a generalization assumes repetition.

It is clear, then, that *history deals with past social facts,* but it is important to note that *all past social facts are not necessarily historical facts.* The terms historical and social are not synonymous. A past social fact becomes an historical fact when it has been made a part of an historical synthesis, for *historical, when applied to human affairs, signifies nothing less than a certain logical way of looking at and organizing past social facts.* When our attention is directed toward the *uniqueness,* the *individuality* of past social facts, when they interest because of their importance for the *unique evolution of man in his activities as a social being,* in selecting the facts and in grouping them into a complex, evolving whole, we employ the historical method; the result of our work is history.

If, on the contrary, we are interested in *what past social facts have in common,* in the way in which *social facts repeat themselves,* if our purpose is to form *generalizations, or laws* concerning social activities, we employ another logical method, the method of the natural sciences. We select our facts not for their individuality or for the importance of their individuality for a complex whole, but for what each fact has in common with others and *the synthesis is not a complex, unique whole, but a generalization in which no trace of the individuality of the past social fact remains*. The result of our work is sociology, not history. Thus the work of the historian supplements that of the sociologist. *The historian is interested in quality, individuality, uniqueness; the sociologist in quantity, in generalization, in repetition.*

Sociology cannot, then, be the science of history; it is the natural science of society. Both the historian and the sociologist deal with past social facts, but not always with the same past social facts, nor in selecting and grouping the facts do they employ the same methods. *Their methods are logically different, because their ends are different.* This difference between the synthesis of history and that of sociology, or the natural science of society, may be crudely illustrated by a figure. Before us, upon a table, lie a large number of pieces of colored glass of different sizes, shapes and colors. The problem is to form from these fragments a single sheet of glass the size of the table top. It may be solved in two ways. The pieces may be thrown into a melting pot and when completely fused the molten mass may be poured into a mould the size of the table top. When the glass has cooled, we shall have a single sheet of glass of uniform color. The individual pieces have, however, disappeared. In vain we look for that bit of orange or crimson of peculiar shape; it has lost its individuality in a composite whole. But there is another way of solving the problem of unity. Bit by bit the fragments might be fitted together until each piece had found its place and a complex whole, a stained-glass window, has been called into being. The pieces have not lost their individuality, but retain it as parts of a larger, complex, unique whole. The first process is that of natural science, of sociology; the second, that of history.

From this brief account of the logic of historical as distinguished from sociological synthesis, it should be clear that sociology does not rest upon a substratum of history, but that both history and sociology rest upon a foundation of past social facts, approach these facts from different points of view, employ logically different methods in selecting and combining the facts and attain logically different syntheses. If this be true, the suggestion that the synthesis of sociology be substituted for that of history, on the ground that history is thus "raised to the rank of a science," would, if adopted, tend to confound things that should be kept distinct. Both syntheses are justifiable, and both are scientific.

The entire reality may, in a word, be studied and organized from the point of view of the general, of repetition, of law, or, as we say, nature. This method, applied to ever widening fields of research, gives us sociology, psychology, biology, chemistry, physics and mechanics. The more comprehensive the generalization, the less of quality it contains, until the climax is reached in a law of motion applied to units from which quality has been completely eliminated. This method of natural science is as old as language. We note its beginning in the use of such terms as man, woman, tree, house, clothing, law, king, queen, government and thousands of others. We call them common nouns, or terms applied to groups of objects, calling attention to some common characteristic. The term clothing, for example, is applied to all objects used as covering for the body, but the word suggests nothing as to the texture, color, shape or size of the covering.

All reality can, on the other hand, be organized from the point of view of difference, of individuality, or uniqueness, in other words, from the historical point of view. The beginning of the historical point of view is likewise as old as language; its concepts we term proper nouns. Mary, John, the Charter Oak, the White House, are terms calling attention not to what an object has in common with others, but to what differentiates it from other objects, to what constitutes its individuality, its uniqueness. And when applied to incidents, to actions, the terms emphasize likewise the unique. It is the battle of *Waterloo,* the *German* reformation, the *French* revolution that is of interest, and not all *battles,* all *reformations* and all *revolutions*. Moreover, the whole with which the historical point of view deals is not a *generalization*, but a *complex whole*, the complexity and individuality increasing with the size of the whole. The history of the Greek people is more complex than the battle of Marathon, which is only a part of it; but the history of the Greek people, in its turn, is less complex than the history of Europe, of which it forms a part. World history —the last great, complex whole—is more complex than any of its parts, because it embraces them all.

If science is organized knowledge, then both natural science and history are scientific; they represent the complete organization of reality from two different logical points of view. "From one to the other no bridge leads." An historical incident can not be deduced from a natural law. That is, the burning of Moscow cannot be deduced from our general knowledge of the law of combustion, nor can a law of natural science be built up on an historical incident, upon what has happened but once and never can happen again in exactly the same way. When the sociologist makes use of the work of the historian, he destroys the complex whole, using the raw material for new and different ends.

Natural science cannot, then, give us an exhaustive knowledge of reality; a knowledge of history, of reality organized from the point of view of the unique, is equally essential. As limited to human affairs, history concerns itself with the complex, unique evolution of man in his activities as a social being. It begins with the first traces of social life and will end only when society itself disappears from the earth. The necessity of such knowledge to the individual should be self-evident. Man is a dependent member of a living social organization. This social organization is the product of all the social life that has preceded it, the last chapter in a continuous drama in many scenes and acts. Effective action by an individual, as a member of society, depends not solely upon a knowledge of the life of his own time, but likewise upon that of the preceding ages out of which his own age has developed. If he would understand the problems of his own age, he must study them as parts of the great, unique evolution of the human race. He must possess a full, detailed and exact knowledge of that unique evolution. Such knowledge can be obtained only by historical study. This vicarious experience, undergone by past generations, supplements the experience of the living present and is quite as indispensable. The octogenarian of wide and varied experience sadly deceives himself, if he imagines that his large personal experience can in any way serve as a substitute for the experience obtained from historical study. Individual experience develops the consciousness of the individual; the study of the past of humanity develops the historical consciousness of the race.

That a generation may know the past, the history of the past must be written and taught. It is a striking fact that the leading peoples of the world, those displaying the most highly developed historical consciousness, possess the largest number of historians, have the greatest output of historical work and devote the largest amount of time to the teaching of history in the schools. The writing and teaching of history does for the race what living does for the individual; it acquaints it with the experience of the race. It is necessary, then, that history should be both written and taught. In truth, it always has been taught. When the half-savage man recited to his child the deeds of his ancestors, history was being recorded and historical consciousness was being developed. The distance that separates the age in which we live from those remote days may be shown as clearly by the number of individuals devoting their lives to historical research and by the amount of time given in the schools to historical study as by the complicated social machinery which differentiates the civilization of today from primitive society.

If the knowledge of the past is a necessity, it must be taught to each generation; before it can be taught, it must be written. This reconstructed experience of the past, if it is to be valuable, must be full, detailed and above all exact. Hence, the first consideration in an historical narration is not picturesqueness or a pleasing style, but truth; a sound historical consciousness can rest on no other foundation. Assuming that a knowledge of the past is a necessity, how can it be acquired? What is the historical process, the method of reconstructing the past? History has been written for centuries, but a conscious study and formulation of the method used by the historian in reconstructing the past is a matter of recent date. Bernheim's *Lehrbuch der historischen Methode* (1889) was the first attempt to describe the method in detail and to supply the student of historical research with a full and reliable manual. Here was gathered up and presented in systematic form the accumulated experience of the historians of the past as learned from a study of their works or from what they had written about their methods of research. Historical investigation had at last become fully conscious.

The process by which the historical past is reconstructed differs fundamentally from the method of natural science. Natural science establishes its generalizations by experimentation. Because it is not interested in the individual—the unique—it can eliminate this element from the problem, thus rendering experimentation, or repetition, possible. It is observed that certain causes, working under certain conditions, seemingly produce certain results. Again and again these causes may be set at work under like conditions, and the effect observed until it is possible to state with certainty what the outcome will be, that is, to predict it. *It should be noted, however, that prediction in natural science has nothing historical in it; natural science cannot predict the unique.* It may teach us the conditions under which combustion will *always* take place, but it cannot tell us that those conditions existed in Moscow in 1812, and will exist again in some other place on a given day. Because he is interested in the unique, the historian can not take advantage of experimentation. He cannot conjure up the figures of the past and cause them to reproduce for him the famous scenes of history. *History never repeats itself,* and it is from what remains from the *single act* that this act must be reproduced. The student of natural science may study actual changes taking place before his eyes, may observe them directly, may reproduce them; *the historian sees not the fact, but only the residue of the fact, and from a study of this he attempts to reconstruct the fact itself. This residue of the historical past we call sources. Without sources, no part of the historical past can be reconstructed.*

The historical sources are the remains of man's unique activities as a social being. One large part of them was not originally intended to supply information to the historian, but because of its origin, because it was the product of historical activities, it is fitted to supply information concerning these activities. This group is infinite in number and variety. Here we encounter the remains of the human body, of clothing, food, dwellings, arms, utensils, books, pictures, statuary, language, literature, laws, manners and customs. To this group of sources the technical term *remains* is given. These objects may be

observed directly and inferences drawn from them
touching the manners and customs of the times in
which they originated. Concerning the evolution of
the unique activities of the period to which they belong, they say little, and it is to a second division of
sources, called *tradition,* that we must turn for the
information not found in remains. A tradition is a
record of the impression made upon some human
brain by a past event and was intended at the time
of its origin to convey information concerning that
event. The record of the impression may be oral,
written or pictorial. A large part of our history is
necessarily reconstructed from written tradition, containing not the fact itself, but what the witness
thought the fact was.

The first step taken by the historian in the attempt to reconstruct man's unique social past is to
bring together all the sources that can be discovered
containing any information on the period under investigation. Once collected, the sources must be submitted to a rigorous criticism to determine the value
of the affirmations in each tradition and the relation
of the affirmations to each other. *For historical
truth is established by the agreement of the affirmations of well-informed, independent witnesses.* After
the facts have been established, they are grouped
in logical and chronological order to form a complex whole, and a narrative, based on the outline
and accompanied by notes in proof of the affirmations contained in the text, completes the work of

the historian. In a word, the process is this: the historical event takes place and leaves its deposit of sources behind it; the historian collects the sources, criticises them, compares the affirmations contained in the traditions, groups the facts and writes his narrative.

The value of the reconstruction, of the narrative, depends obviously upon (1) the quantity and quality of the sources and (2) upon the critical skill and constructive ability of the historian, or, in other words, upon his knowledge of historical method. This knowledge of method is of value to the general student of history as well as to the specialist. If education consists quite as much in a knowledge of the processes by which we attain to truth as in the knowledge of truth itself, acquaintance with the method of investigation in history should form part of the training of every student in history. Laboratory work in the natural sciences is taken as a matter of course today; its justification is found not in the amount of information acquired, but in the value of the knowledge of the method by which truth is ascertained in the natural sciences. And yet the method, once learned, is, as a rule, used only by the specialist. We may know how to detect impurities in water, but we turn the work over to a trained bacteriologist.

Every hour in the day, however, we are forced to pass judgments upon the truth or falsity of historical events, to apply the tests of historical method. The work is done, as a rule, unconsciously and crudely. Why not make it conscious and scientific? Recently the people of two continents were called upon to decide between the rival claims of Cook and Peary. It was a problem in historical criticism, not to be solved by the knowledge of a mass of historical data, but by an acquaintance with the method of handling historical evidence and with the process by which historical facts are established. The public was quite incapable of dealing with it. But it is not simply in estimating the truth or falsity of contemporary history that a knowledge of historical method proves itself a valuable part of the equipment of an educated person. A knowledge of the method is likewise the Ariadne thread which will guide him through the maze of secondary historical works—many of little value—constantly pouring from the press.

A knowledge of the theory of historical method and some acquaintance with its application do not form the sole preparation for historical research and for the teaching of history. A few practical suggestions to the undergraduate specializing in history or to the teacher who wishes to become a trained specialist will form a fitting conclusion to this introduction.

First among the indispensable aids to historical study, especially the study of European history, is a knowledge of language. The investigator must be able to read his sources in the language in which they were written and he must also be able to read secondary works upon the period he is investigating whether printed in English, French, German or Italian. The first-hand study of Greek, Roman or mediaeval history calls for a knowledge of Greek and Latin, to make the sources accessible, and of French, German and Italian for the reading of modern writers. The necessity of acquiring a knowledge of Latin grows less as we advance into modern history, but in dealing with the history of the church it never entirely disappears. The language equipment that may be required of a writer of the history of Europe in the nineteenth century is something appalling. It may call for a reading knowledge not only of the Germanic and Romance languages,—German, Dutch, Swedish, Norwegian, Danish, French, Italian, Spanish and Portuguese,—but of Greek, Magyar, Russian and Turkish, enough to make the boldest hesitate. This is not, however, an impossible task for one who begins his language study early and keeps at it persistently.

One should decide as early as possible in what field of history one's interest lies. Whether one decides for ancient or modern history, a reading knowledge of German and French and, if possible, of Italian, should be acquired in the undergraduate years and this knowledge at once put to use in historical reading and research. Two years of German and one year of French should be the minimum amount of language taken in the classroom, if the student would not be seriously handicapped in his subsequent work. But the classroom work in language will have been thrown away, if it is not persistently followed up by the use of historical works in German and French. To do this is not easy, but it must be done, if historical scholarship is the end in view. The important thing is to use the languages constantly until they can be used readily.

A second subject that should be studied in undergraduate years in connection with history is literature. And here likewise the simple classroom work will not suffice. In general, the student should read —not necessarily in the original language—the masterpieces of the great literatures, as expressions of the spiritual ideals and cravings of the peoples. He should read more intensively in the literature of the people and of the period in which his historical interest centers. A few of the best English and French works on literary criticism should form a part of his reading. Much may be accomplished in the four undergraduate years, if a definite program is prepared and followed systematically. The work thus begun should be carried on during the years of graduate study.

The study of art and architecture should accompany the study of literature. A few good volumes on architecture, sculpture and painting should be carefully read as guides to the examination of photographs of works of art, of facsimiles or, in the case of paintings, of the originals themselves when they are accessible in a gallery. One year to Greek art, one to the art of the Renaissance and one to the art of the nineteenth century would make a fair beginning. The time should not be wasted on unimportant works and unimportant men, but the great men and their works should be dwelt on sufficiently long to make a lasting impression possible and to enable the student to acquire a sympathetic acquaintance with the masterpieces of the men who have set the standard in the world of art.

A course in logic, dealing with the theory of knowledge and the classification of the sciences, is essential. It will enable the student to understand the place of history among the sciences and will save him from the mental unrest that so many have passed through in the fruitless attempt to transform history into a natural science. This course in logic should be followed by a course in the philosophy of history and by the study of the principal works of James, Eucken and Bergson. To the historian, a philosophy of life is indispensable as a prerequisite to a concept of world history.

Language, literature, art, logic, philosophy are all directly related to the work of the historian in his attempt to trace the unique evolution of man in his activities as a social being. Another group of subjects dealing with social repetitions or laws—economics, political science, psychology and sociology —is of indirect value for the student of history and at least an elementary knowledge of each should be acquired.

[30]

INTRODUCTION

The historical study proper should run through the four undergraduate years. General surveys of ancient, mediaeval, and modern history—including English and American—should be followed by more intensive studies of limited periods. The aim in these latter studies should be not only to learn something of the history of a period, but also to make the acquaintance of the principal sources and secondary works relating to it. These works should be actually handled and certain parts read. The secondary works should be carefully chosen, no time being wasted upon works once famous, still occupying a place in our libraries, but scientifically out of date. A speaking acquaintance should be made with the most important historical reviews.

Parallel with the general historical work should go the intensive or method work. It should be begun in the first year and should be based in the first two years on sources in English or translated into English; in the last two years sources in the original languages—Latin, French, German—may be used. After four years of careful, scientific, intensive work the student will be prepared to do graduate work of some value.

If the student is interested in European history, his dream and his plans will be to go to Europe to study. He will act wisely, if he defers this graduate study until he has received his master's degree from some one of the leading universities in this country, has decided on his special field of work, has a reading knowledge of the European language he will be called upon to use, knows what critical work means, has done all that can be done in this country on his thesis and is ready to profit by what he finds on the continent. What he should hope to acquire in Europe is a speaking knowledge of at least one language; a knowledge of the life of at least one of the European peoples; the assistance of the man who knows more than any other man about the subject in which he is interested and an opportunity to examine the sources, both printed and manuscript, which are necessary for the completion of the investigation he has begun on this side of the Atlantic.

What has been suggested here as preparation for historical study is far beyond what the great majority of history teachers have enjoyed, but is within the reach of all teachers of average ability who will set themselves seriously and systematically to work. Four or five years of patient, continuous study, in accordance with a well-arranged program, can accomplish wonders. It is worth doing, for it puts enthusiasm into the teacher's work and keeps him alive intellectually. Nothing contributes more to these ends than research work. How that work may be begun and carried on, it is the purpose of this volume to show.

II

CHOICE OF A SUBJECT.
COLLECTION AND CLASSIFICATION
OF SOURCES

THE first problem which confronts the beginner in research work is the choice of a subject. It does not present itself in the same way to the undergraduate as to the advanced student. To the undergraduate, who is learning the technique of method, the question as to whether the topic selected for study has been worked over before is a matter of no great importance. The same laboratory problems are assigned in chemistry, botany and physics year after year. The fact that these problems had all been solved by scientists before they were used for elementary work in no way lessens their value for such work. The training in method, in technique, is the purpose of the work, not *original* research.

The topic in history for beginners should be assigned by the instructor and the source material put into the hands of the students. I know this runs counter to the common practice. It eliminates the bibliographical work from the first year and stresses the second step in research, the critical handling of evidence. Much can be said, however, in favor of this change. To run over a card catalogue, a periodical index or a volume of bibliography and note the titles of books or articles bearing on a given topic is not a difficult matter. The technique is learned in the first hour of work; after that, it is largely repetition, and the titles might quite as well be gathered by proxy and presented to the student. A large part of the material thus collected is of no value whatever for the scientific historical worker. The gathering and reading of worthless material is time thrown away, time that could be given with much greater advantage to the critical study of valuable source material. If we cannot, in the first year of college work, teach both bibliography and criticism, let us teach criticism; bibliography can be taught later in the course.

While it is not necessary to lay an original problem before beginners, it is quite as easy as to present one that has been thoroughly worked over and the original problem is much more interesting both for the instructor and for the class. The same problem should be assigned to the whole class, if it is to be made the basis for classroom study, as it should be. If the interest of the instructor lies in a field for which no printed source studies exist, it is no great task to arrange a study. Forty or fifty pages of sources supply material enough for the purpose and this may be put out in mimeographed sheets at slight expense to the student.

For the advanced student, for one who has taken his first steps in research and is looking about for original work to do, the problem presents itself in a different form. It is not a question of what one would *like to do,* but of what one is *able to do,* of what *needs to be done* and of *what can be done.* As the result of his reading, a student or teacher may have become interested in a topic in Greek or Russian history. He would like to investigate it, to write it up from the sources. Can he read Greek and Latin, or Russian? He cannot. Is he willing to learn to read them in order to be able to do this work? He had not thought of it and on considering the matter seriously decides that it would be unwise to undertake it. Perhaps he has been attracted by some topic in the Middle Ages, but has no knowledge of mediaeval Latin, paleography or diplomatics, all of which he should know as preliminary to the study of the sources.

If the student is young, the interest in the topic great and the topic worth the time and trouble, the preparation may be acquired and the work executed; for the older student, who has no time to spare, it would be better to seek a subject in a field which may be worked with the preparation he already has or that may be acquired without too great expenditure of time and effort. It is better, if possible, to select a subject for investigation from some field in which the student is somewhat widely read, for no topic can be successfully investigated, if the investigator does not possess a good working background for it. To acquire such a background one must devote much time to the reading of secondary histories. Much of this time can be saved, if a topic is chosen in a familiar field.

Two very important suggestions to the beginner are (1) to limit the scope of the investigation so that the work may be thoroughly done in the time that may be given to it and (2) to select a topic that is a part of a larger whole, making possible an indefinite continuation of research. Young students left to themselves might choose the whole subject of the diplomatic history of the Thirty Years' War, or of reconstruction in the South, without any conception of the number of years it would take to examine the sources upon which such a thesis, if it is to be of any scientific value, must rest. A single episode of the first subject or an account of reconstruction in a single state will give occupation enough for the graduate student. When, on the other hand, a student selects a topic that is isolated, that connects with nothing larger, he runs the risk of ending his investigations with his master's or doctor's thesis.

Finally, it is well to avoid topics for the investigation of which the student has no natural fitness or taste. Problems from economic, religious or art history, for example, should not be undertaken unless the student has some natural taste for such matters and can approach them sympathetically.

If the student is able to investigate the subject, the next question is, Does it need to be investigated? In other words: (1) Has it never been investigated?

(2) Has it been investigated in an incomplete way? (3) Has the material been treated uncritically? (4) Is a new and valuable synthesis possible? (5) Has new material been found that justifies the re-examination of the topic? If one or more of these conditions exist, the topic needs to be investigated. But how can one be certain that any one of these conditions does exist? A quick way to find out is to consult some historian who knows, somebody who is a specialist in the field in which the student is interested. If no such person can be found, the student must solve the problem himself. To discover what has been written on the topic is a bibliographical problem; to determine whether the writers of these works have utilized all the existing source material is also a bibliographical problem; to pass judgment upon the manner in which the sources have been used is a critical problem; and, finally, to decide whether the facts can be combined in a new and instructive way is a problem in synthesis. How these problems should be dealt with will be shown later.

While answering the second problem,—the need of investigation,—the student will have acquired the means of answering the third, Can the topic be investigated? In other words, are there sources enough in existence to enable the investigator to determine what the historical facts were? If not, no matter how interesting the topic may be, it cannot be investigated.

The topic for investigation having been fixed

upon, the next step is to collect the material with which the investigation is to deal, that is to say, the secondary works and the sources. The secondary works are often helpful in indicating what the sources are, in interpreting and criticising them, in establishing the facts and in synthesizing them. Not to take advantage of all the good work done in the past on the topic would clearly be a waste of time and an indication of a lack of understanding of the right conditions of scientific advance. Each generation of historians should begin where the previous generation left off, and each historian should work with posterity in view and formulate the result of his work in such a way that it will not be necessary to do it over again.

To learn what has been written on a topic in European history is no easy matter. Bibliographies of countries and periods can be found, but they may not be sufficiently exhaustive in their lists, or may not have been published at a sufficiently recent date, so that one is not certain that they tell the whole story. Furthermore, such bibliographies deal almost, if not quite, wholly with books and tell us nothing of what has been printed in historical reviews. There is a long list of such reviews, English, French, German, Italian, Russian, etc., any one of which may contain a satisfactory treatment of the topic which has been selected for investigation, thus making a new treatment unnecessary. It is not safe to go ahead without examining at least the indexes of the reviews of the country of whose history the topic forms a part. As a rule it is wise to do more than this. In the last few years, for example, perhaps as much has been published in Russian reviews on the France of the late eighteenth century as in French reviews. The German reviews have also had some valuable studies on the same period.

As the bibliographical work proceeds, the student should form a card catalogue of the titles, examine the works and take notes upon any matter he may want to make use of. If the notes are at all voluminous, it is better to keep them apart from the catalogue in a loose-leaved notebook. A card is well enough for a brief note, but a sheet of paper should be used for a long extract.

Up to a certain point the preparation of a bibliography of the sources does not differ from that of secondary works. In searching for secondary works, however, we are searching for printed matter, while this may be true of the search for sources to a limited extent only. A large part of the sources may be in manuscript form, some of them may be oral and pictorial, while some may belong to the group called remains. Of a large part of this material, no bibliographical trace may exist. To discover the material is a most important part of the work of the investigator. *For a thorough search for sources, a serious attempt to bring together all the evidence bearing upon the topic* is the *sine qua non* of a piece of investigation that is to have any permanent value.

To succeed in this search for unrecorded evidence one must have both ingenuity and patience; ingenuity in forming hypotheses concerning the existence and probable location of evidence and patience in testing these hypotheses. In a large majority of cases, the search is fruitful. For example, a trial of some importance for a topic under investigation took place in London in 1785. The only evidence hitherto used in dealing with the incident had been an account published at the time in a London paper. More and better sources were wanted. What would they be? Court records naturally. What was the court? The Old Bailey, which still exists. Have the records for 1785 been preserved? From a visit to the court it is learned that a stenographic account of the trials was published in 1785, and a copy of this record was found in the Guild Hall library.

On another occasion the investigator was interested in an incident that took place in Holland. A Frenchman had been extradited at the request of the government of Louis XVI. The incident had been written up wholly from French sources. Do no Dutch sources exist? The arrest was made in Amsterdam. The council of Amsterdam would be obliged to correspond with the government at The Hague. Doubtless material could be found in the city archives of Amsterdam and in the state archives at The Hague. Inquiry at these two places brought the documents to light. A somewhat different case would be where one knew that certain material had existed,—a newspaper, for example,—but did not know where it could be found. A search in one of the great libraries of Europe, London or Paris, would probably lead to the discovery of a copy.

Oral tradition should be sought for in the place where the incident took place and with the aid of the local antiquarian. He may have discovered the material needed, but the knowledge of his discovery may never have gone beyond the bounds of the town. In the search for material, one thing leads to another, sometimes in the most extraordinary way. One summer, some years ago, I visited Aix-en-Provence for the purpose of making the acquaintance of M. Guibal, professor in the University of Aix, who had written a very exhaustive and scholarly work on Mirabeau and the Provence. M. Guibal was not in the city, but a gentleman of whom I inquired, on learning of my mission, introduced me to M. Mouttet, who for years had been a student of the life of Mirabeau in Provence and was full of valuable information. He, in his turn, made me acquainted with M. Paul Arbaud, who had in his possession a large number of important Mirabeau manuscripts hitherto unused by the biographers of Mirabeau.

These illustrations may give some slight idea of the way in which source material is brought to light when no trace of it exists in printed bibliographies. It may be well to add that the search for sources does not end until the printed work comes from the press. The discovery of fresh material may take place while the narrative is being written and necessitate the recasting of a large part of the text. The path of research is a rocky one and not always pleasant to travel.

In working over his manuscript sources, or rare printed matter, the young investigator is apt to content himself with notes giving the substance of the source. That method is often a bad one. When the time comes to use the notes, the investigator may be far from his sources and it may be absolutely necessary to know the exact wording of the text. It is much wiser to make extracts in the exact language of the document, and when there is the slightest doubt as to whether certain parts should be omitted or not, to copy the whole document. It is safer in the long run. Another suggestion for the beginner, whose time may be limited when he is abroad for research work, is to make use of a copyist. When the material has been found and it is simply a matter of copying it, the investigator cannot afford to give his time to it when a copyist will do the work even better and for a few cents a page.

Something has already been written about the nature of material used in the reconstruction of the historical past. It is as varied as human activities. To enumerate it all would be impossible; the labor would be of doubtful utility. For the effective use of the sources, it is important to know the main divisions and subdivisions employed by the writers on method in the classification of the sources and the reasons for this classification. The two main divisions are *remains* and *tradition*. The ground for this division is readily understood.

The first group comprises all objects coming down to us from the past, actual products of man's social activities. They came into existence as the result of man's daily needs and *were not created for the purpose of acquainting posterity with the nature of man's activities*. If these objects later found their way into museums, such a disposition of them was not anticipated by their creators. Sources of this kind, infinite in variety as they are, ranging from different kinds of breakfast food, through clothing, buildings, machinery, works of literature and art to the most trivial ornaments of human vanity, can supply us with but a small part of the information we need concerning man's unique social evolution. They reveal to us the results of actions, not actions themselves. To interpret these remains is a most difficult process, yielding, often, very questionable results. It will be remembered what a false fabric of inference concerning the Aryan race was built upon the uncertain foundation of the common root words in the European and Indian languages. The fabric has been demolished, not because the common root words do not exist, but because their existence did not justify the inferences drawn from them. With this class of sources, the beginner will have little to do. A detailed treatment of them will be found in Bernheim's work.

The second group of sources is called tradition. Some of these, from one point of view, might be treated as remains, but the significant characteristic of the group, the characteristic which distinguishes it from remains proper, is the fact that it contains the records of the impressions made upon human brains by man's social activities. The events took place, someone saw them and made a record of what he thought he saw, and that record has been handed down to us. It may be preserved in three ways, by word of mouth, in writing, or pictorially, and thus we have oral, written and pictorial tradition. Oral tradition, after a time, may disappear or become written tradition, so that in the end the forms of the record are chiefly two and more largely written than oral. In the present generation, through the use of photography, the volume and value of the pictorial record have been very much increased.

In the first division of sources,—remains,—we can see the actual objects that have come down to us from past times; in the second,—tradition,—containing the impressions made upon individual minds by man's past activities, *what we see is not the act, but what the witness thought the act was.*

In dealing with a tradition, it must be remembered that at least one human brain stands between us and the fact. We can see the fact only indirectly. In dealing with the affirmation of a witness,—which may be something quite different from the fact itself,—in trying to determine how true the affirmation is, we must always keep the personality of the witness in view. This profound difference between remains and tradition inevitably gives rise to a difference of method in handling the two groups of sources. But the value of the tradition is determined not alone by the personality of the witness; the character of the sources must also be taken into consideration.

The division of tradition into three groups rests upon the manner in which the tradition is formulated. It is not a matter of scientific indifference whether the tradition is passed on orally, in writing, or pictorially. The value of the affirmation is affected by the form in which it expresses itself. The first account of what the witness has seen, if formulated at once, may be as valuable in the oral as in the written form. But this is not true when the affirmation is repeated. If the impression is committed to writing, it is fixed and not injuriously affected by lack of memory; oral tradition is fluid, each repetition differing more and more from the original, until, in time, the affirmation becomes practically worthless. This is true whether the affirmation is repeated year after year by the original witness, or is passed on from individual to individual. Oral tradition is, then, as a class, much less reliable than written tradition.

Pictorial tradition occupies a middle ground between oral and written tradition. The impression made by an individual or by a scene upon the artist is fixed on canvas or in marble; in this respect—its fixity—pictorial tradition resembles written tradition. It differs from it in the greater difficulty offered by the medium—paint or marble—and the greater completeness with which the record must be made. The result is that there are greater possibilities of error in the pictorial record than in the written. The written record cannot, however, take the place of the pictorial record. No written description of Washington could give us the same clear conception of his personal appearance that could be obtained from an excellent portrait or statue by a contemporary artist.

Written tradition itself may be divided into numerous groups, differing from each other in value. The same event—for example, a scene in the great French assembly of 1789—may be described in the minutes of the assembly (*Procès-verbal*), in a newspaper, in a pamphlet, in a letter of a member to his constituents, in a letter of another member to his wife, in a letter of a diplomat residing in Paris at the time, or in the *Mémoires* of a member. Here are five groups of material, official records, newspapers, pamphlets, letters and *Mémoires,* differing from each other in value because of the character of the source. The experienced investigator understands the general valuation to put upon each. Diplomatic correspondence intended for publication, party programs, political speeches, war bulletins, illustrate some of the groups of written tradition which are notoriously untrustworthy. Something will be said in a later chapter of the way in which these groups are evaluated. At present, it is only necessary to point out that the reason for classifying the sources, instead of leaving them a heterogeneous mass, is to enable the historian to determine more readily the value of the individual sources, by knowing the value of the class to which they belong.

Having selected a subject for investigation, collected and classified the sources, the next step in the process is the criticism of the sources for the purpose of determining the value of the evidence they contain and the relation of the different witnesses to each other.

III

CRITICISM OF THE SOURCES: GENUINENESS

THE sources collected for the purpose of restoring the historical past do not contain the facts, but the affirmations of witnesses concerning the facts. The *fact* is what actually took place; the *affirmation* is a statement by a witness of what he *believed* took place. *The fact is established by the agreement of two or more independent witnesses.* Before, however, the affirmations in the different sources can be used to establish the fact, each source must be evaluated and the relationship of the sources to each other must be studied to determine whether they are dependent or independent. There is nothing novel in this procedure; it is simply the method of every day rendered conscious and precise. The man on the street does not receive the testimony of every witness with equal confidence, but in a rough and ready way puts a value upon the statements of each. The historian has carefully considered the reasons for trusting or distrusting the affirmations of a witness and has arranged these reasons in an orderly manner, together with the tests to be applied to the sources.

If much of the work of historians in the past has

had no permanent value because of the failure to base it upon exhaustive research, as much more has been discarded because it showed little or no trace of the critical evaluation of the sources. The one is as indispensable as the other. *All the sources on a topic must be collected and all must be critically evaluated.* Such work consumes a vast amount of time and only a limited topic can be investigated, but what of that? The end of scientific historical work is reliable, scientific results, and nothing obliges the investigator to undertake more than he can do thoroughly. Scientific historical work is the only kind worth while, the only kind which makes progress in historical reconstruction possible. Let the young investigator set his standards high and then limit the scope of his work so that it will be possible to live up to the standards he has set. When he has once learned what excellent work means, he will be content with nothing less, if he be animated by the true spirit of scholarship.

The whole problem of the evaluation of a source is one of the relation of the witness to the fact reported. It resolves itself into certain minor problems: (1) Is the source genuine or is it a forgery? (2) Who wrote it and when and where was it written? (3) Do all the affirmations contained in the source relate to the witness's own observations or are some of them hearsay? (4) In the latter case, where was the information obtained? (5) Finally, all these questions having been answered, what is the value of such a source?

Naturally the first test to which a source must be subjected is that for genuineness. If it is a forgery, that is, not what it pretends to be, either in whole or in part (interpolation), it clearly cannot be used as evidence. To the uninitiated or credulous there would seem to be little opportunity today for the exercise of scepticism concerning the genuineness of the sources of modern history. All the well-known forgeries are supposed to be ancient affairs, and the assumption is that we have left forgeries behind us, together with the stage-coach. Unfortunately that is not so. To forge successfully is more difficult today than in the credulous Middle Ages, but motives for forgeries still exist and the only protection against them is eternal vigilance. *Every bit of evidence should be critically scanned before it is accepted as genuine.* And it must be remembered that the document as a whole may be genuine, but may contain a forged interpolated portion.

Forged material is found in all the groups of sources, in remains as well as in the various kinds of tradition. Every traveller knows to his sorrow how wide-spread and difficult of detection the activity of the forger is in works of art and relics. Antique rugs, vases, paintings, statuary, bronzes, are so skilfully reproduced that even the connoisseur may be deceived. I was once told by a distinguished French sculptor who was a collector of Greek vases that the modern reproductions, passed off for originals, were often so good that he could settle the question of genuineness only by scratching the clay. Collections of ancient pottery and of parchments have been sold for large sums to museums; later investigation has shown that they were skilful forgeries. Two of the most famous cases are those of the Moabite pottery and the Sardinian manuscripts.

After the discovery in 1866, in the land of Moab, of the Mesa stone with its valuable inscription, there were offered for sale by a dealer in antiques in Jerusalem certain old Hebrew inscriptions similar to that on the Mesa stone. In the spring of 1872, there appeared at the same place certain pieces of pottery and, later in the year, vases, urns, etc., with inscriptions and drawings. There were 2,000 pieces in all. The articles had been brought to Jerusalem by an Arab, Selim, who had been in the employ of European excavators. The dealer in Jerusalem, charged with fraud, went to the place indicated by Selim, in company with those interested, and found other articles of a like nature. Although criticism was not silenced, many of the objects were bought for the Berlin museum. Careful criticism has shown that the articles are counterfeits, probably the work of Selim.

The Sardinian forgery is even more interesting. In the years 1863 to 1865, there were published in Italy letters, biographies, poems and other literary fragments, supposed to have been composed on the island of Sardinia, in the period from the eighth cen-

ST. IGNATIUS HOUSE OF STUDIES
LIBRARY
MANHASSET

tury to the fifteenth. The find created a great sensation, for it was not supposed that such a state of culture had ever existed in Sardinia. After publication, the originals were deposited in the library at Cagliari. A heated discussion having arisen in Italy over the genuineness of the material, some of the originals were submitted to the Academy of Sciences at Berlin for examination. Jaffé investigated the material of the manuscripts and the handwriting; Tobler, the language and literature; Dove, the historical contents. They established beyond the possibility of a doubt that the material was forged.

The Forged Decretals, the Gift of Constantine, the poems of Ossian and Chatterton, are forgeries known to every schoolboy. The list might be extended almost indefinitely. Those wishing to pursue the matter further should consult Bernheim, where additional illustrations and references to the literature of the subject will be found.

The student of modern history is much more likely to encounter forgeries in the subgroup of written tradition than elsewhere. Very recent examples and very interesting ones, illustrating the necessity of being at all times on one's guard, are the third volume of the *Mémoires* of Bailly, *The Journal of a Spy in Paris during the Reign of Terror,* and the letters of Marie Antoinette.

The third volume of the *Mémoires* of Bailly was not supposed to be the work of Bailly himself. It bore the title, *Supplément aux Mémoires de Bailly* and appeared for the first time in the folio edition of Bailly's *Mémoires* published in 1804, with the title *Avant-Moniteur*. The title-page further announced that the volume was made up of material drawn from "the unpublished notes of the late M. ———, member of the constituent assembly." In a footnote in the folio edition, it was stated that "the author of these notes [was] a witness at Versailles of the exciting scenes within the assembly and of the criminal and thoughtless measures which prepared the insurrection of October 5 and 6." When the *Mémoires* were reprinted in 1822 by Berville and Barriere in three volumes under the title *Mémoires* of Bailly, this anonymous volume constituted the third volume. In the histories of the French revolution written since 1822, the edition of Bailly's *Mémoires* of that date is made use of and the third volume is referred to as if it were the work of Bailly. Although the work was anonymous, there was no suspicion that it might be a forgery.

No serious attempt was made to determine the authorship of the volume, M. Tourneux suggesting, however, in his bibliography of Paris during the revolution, that it might be the work of Camus, a member of the assembly.

That was the status of the case when I began the examination of the volume with a class of undergraduates, hoping to solve the problem of authorship. The volume was written in the form of a diary, giving day by day an account of what took place in the assembly. I assigned a certain number of paragraphs to different members of the class, asking them to compare the text with the text of contemporary daily papers which reported the proceedings of the assembly. When the reports were made, it was discovered that a paragraph of the text of the third volume bore a very close resemblance to the text of one of the newspapers, *Le point du jour;* the two were evidently related. Further comparison revealed other passages almost literally the same and a comparison of the text of the volume with the *Courrier de Provence* showed a more surprising situation. Page after page in the third volume of the *Mémoires* and in the *Courrier de Provence* were almost identically the same, the third person of the paper being changed to the first person of the diary. What material was not found in the *Point du jour* and the *Courrier de Provence* was discovered in a third paper, *Les révolutions de Paris.* For these facts, but one explanation was possible; someone had composed this anonymous "diary" by piecing together extracts from the three newspapers. In other words, the third volume was a forgery.

Who had done it and when had it been done? It was noticed that the anonymous volume appeared as a "supplément" to the folio form of Bailly's *Mémoires* published in 1804, with the title *Avant-Moniteur.* That compound word—*Avant-Moniteur* —proved to be the key to the whole situation. The *Moniteur* was a daily newspaper, the first number appearing November 24, 1789. In 1795, the paper being perhaps the most important daily then published and containing in its files a running history of the revolution, it was decided by the publishers to fill the gap in the files between May 5, 1789, the date of the first meeting of the States-General and November 25, 1789, by supplementary numbers, written with the use of source material and printed in the form of the newspaper itself. This was done. In 1804, when the *Mémoires* of Bailly was published, this introductory volume was out of print and it would have been expensive to reprint it. The editors contracted for an edition of the *Mémoires* in folio form, the title-page to bear the additional word *Avant-Moniteur,* or introduction to the *Moniteur.* But the first number of the *Moniteur* appeared November 24, and the last events recorded in the *Mémoires* of Bailly were those of October 2. How could the gap be filled? In the same way in which the old introduction to the *Moniteur* had been composed, by piecing together extracts from newspapers. Had the extracts been pieced together with an indication of the provenance of each, the procedure would have been perfectly regular, but when the editor changed the person from the third to the first, arranged the extracts in the form of a diary and gave them to the world as the "notes" of "a late member of the constituent assembly," he was committing a forgery. Moreover, it was a senseless forgery, for nothing was gained by it. A volume composed of extracts from newspapers would be useful to one to whom the newspapers are not accessible, but no historian would venture to use this forgery composed of extracts. It is useful today as an example of how that sort of thing is done and as a warning to investigators to accept nothing on faith.

The Journal of a Spy in Paris during the Reign of Terror, January-July 1794, by Raoul Hesdin (John Murray, London, 1895), is one of the most daring of modern forgeries. There were circumstances attending its publication which aroused suspicion and led to a critical examination of the book; the editor had withheld both his name and the location of the manuscript, two suspicious circumstances. An examination of the text gave abundant proof that the work was a forgery. Facts were recorded before they occurred, the error of time being sometimes a few days, sometimes as great as six months. No explanation of such premature knowledge could be given except that the work had not been written from day to day, but was a later compilation by an individual who was not sufficiently careful of his dates. The volume was criticised in detail in the *English Historical Review* (July 1896), and the charge of forgery was made. The author, still guarding his anonymity, wrote to the *Athenaeum* (March 28, April 18, May 16, 1896), defending himself by very specious arguments, but unsuccessfully. The reason for the publication of such a forgery is not evident. It may have been the work of a practical joker; it may have been a political pamphlet, judging from the closing words of the preface, "can the Englishman who lives, as the late Sir H. Maine said, *in fæce Romuli,* altogether afford in 1895, to neglect the terrible object lesson afforded to him by Paris one hundred and one years ago?" It was written by an Englishman, evidently, by an Englishman who knew much about the French revolution and France, but who was inaccurate in scholarship, although possessing a brilliant imagination.

The successful forgery of letters of famous personages is a lucrative business, as such letters can be sold for a good price. The number of forged letters with the signature of Marie Antoinette is so large as to make the work of her biographers exceedingly difficult. The volumes of her letters published by Hunolstein and Feuillet de Conches contain a large number of forgeries, and led to a careful attempt to make a complete list of the genuine letters. This collection, by La Rocheterie and Beaucourt (Paris, 1895), is the most successful effort yet made to publish a critical collection of the letters of the unfortunate queen. Genuine letters exist, many have been published and some reproduced in facsimile, so that the forger has at his command abundant material to aid him in reproducing both the handwriting and the style. The introduction to the work of La Rocheterie and Beaucourt supplies a valuable account of the methods used in distinguishing genuine letters from forgeries.

[57]

A recent monograph on the early French revolution, by Dr. Otto Becker, furnishes a good illustration of the relation of the problem of genuineness to the value of historical reconstruction. To prove that on June 20, 1789, Marie Antoinette believed that the wisest policy for Louis XVI to follow was to take the side of the third estate, a letter of the queen, written on that day, was quoted. Dr. Becker found the text of the letter in a French work published at Paris in 1858. The collection of letters published in 1896 by La Rocheterie and Beaucourt contains no letter dated June 20, 1789. Is the letter quoted by Dr. Becker genuine? He did not even raise the question. It may be; it may not be. It should be tested.

In the first place, the French work, where the text is found, should be examined to discover, if possible, where the original manuscript is. If no help is to be found in this work, the task of determining the falsity or genuineness of the letter is a difficult one, for it is much more easy to forge a printed letter than a manuscript. In the first case, one must reproduce only the language; in the last, language and handwriting. To reproduce the language is not difficult. From sentences taken from genuine letters, it is possible to construct a letter quite unlike any letter existing. Some of the forgeries of the letters of Marie Antoinette were detected by comparing sentences from the suspected letter with the text of genuine letters. This sort of work can be done, however, only by one familiar with the whole collection, and consumes a vast amount of time. In the second place, if the test of style fails, something may be done toward establishment of the probability of forgery by comparing the views contained in the letters with the general attitude of the queen at the time as learned from other sources. If it is impossible to reconcile these views with her general attitude, the presumption of forgery is raised, although it may not be possible to prove the forgery with certainty.

Besides the cases of forgery already cited, there are many others quite as important. Sometimes the authenticity of sources is questioned for a long time and the question finally left unsettled. At other times, after a long discussion, the evidence may seem to be in favor of the genuineness of the material. The *Mémoires* of Talleyrand, published at Paris in 1891, is an example of the first kind, the so-called "Casket Letters" of Mary Queen of Scots an example of the second. The whole case of the guilt or innocence of the queen rests on the genuineness of these letters; recent investigations make out a very convincing case in favor of their genuineness.

Determining the genuineness of written tradition, letters, *Mémoires,* etc., is not work for a novice. If we have what pretends to be the original manuscript, the task is much less difficult than when we have to work without it. In the first case, we can examine the paper and the handwriting. It is difficult to forge a manuscript in the year 1913 and make the paper look as if it were a hundred years old. It is quite as difficult to reproduce successfully the handwriting of another; for a manuscript of any length, it is practically impossible. A comparison of the forgery with the genuine handwriting of the individual to whom it is attributed generally lays bare the deception. When we have nothing but the printed source, we are obliged to depend on style and content. The forgery of the *Journal,* referred to above, was detected by a study of its contents. The writer knew too much; he was acquainted with events before they took place. It is very difficult, practically impossible, not to make that blunder.

Imagine, for example, that one of us today should attempt to forge the diary of an American soldier in the Philippines, during the first month of active fighting. Before beginning the work, we are well informed about the war, but we must forget all we know about the later events or that later knowledge will reveal itself in the diary we are about to write. Such a total forgetting is impossible and to the skilful eye the deception is visible. The contents can be tested, however, only by one well acquainted with the history of the period.

IV

CRITICISM OF THE SOURCES: LOCALIZATION

To say that a source is genuine, is to say nothing of the value of the affirmations contained in it: a letter written by an idiot or a knave may be genuine, but largely valueless as historical material. On the other hand, a manuscript may have all the earmarks of genuineness, but contain no outward indication of authorship or of time and place of writing. Before it can be used, it must be *localized,* that is to say, it must, if possible, be *assigned to a certain author, writing in a certain place* and *at a certain time.* To illustrate the necessity of this information, suppose that a subject were being investigated and someone offered some important evidence bearing upon it. He was not an eyewitness, but had read somewhere what he reported. He did not know where he had read it, who the author was, nor when or where it had been written. How much weight would a careful investigator attach to such information? It should never be forgotten that the value of the affirmations in a source depends on the *character of the source, on the personality of the witness* (who wrote it?) and the *time* (when written?) and *place* (where written?) of writing. The first problem, that of the character of the source, has been dealt with under the classification of the sources; it remains to treat the last three.

The witness is the medium through whom comes our knowledge of the fact; the better the medium, the better the information. Hence the importance of knowing as much as possible about the writer. In this respect, the work of the historian is more difficult than that of the lawyer in the courtroom, who has the living witness before him. The witness of the historian is often a personage concerning whom it may be possible to learn but little, and yet it is necessary to evaluate his testimony from our knowledge of him. The problem falls into two parts: (1) Who was the witness, that is, what was his name? and (2) What kind of a person was he? The first part is a problem only when the name is not given. How do we determine the authorship? If we have a manuscript, the handwriting may put us on the track of the writer. If the manuscript has been lost, the style may help us, if it is very individual. One would recognize the style of Carlyle almost as readily as Carlyle's rugged face. But suppose neither supplies a clue, what then? We must turn to the contents and endeavor to form an idea of the man from what he has written.

A good illustration is the *Journal d'Adrien Duquesnoy,* published in 1894. The work consists of a series of letters written from Versailles and Paris in

1789 and 1790. Two manuscripts exist, one in the National Library in Paris and the other in a private collection. They are not in the handwriting of Duquesnoy, but interspersed in the letters of the private collection are letters in Duquesnoy's handwriting in which he refers to his "Bulletins." The editor also found some corrections in the handwriting of Duquesnoy on the letters of the private collection. This was his ground for attributing the letters to Duquesnoy. When the publication appeared, the authorship of Duquesnoy was denied for the reason that the letters were not in his handwriting and that the internal evidence indicated that at least the earlier bulletins could not have been written by him. Handwriting is not, of course, a final test of authorship; a letter may have been dictated or copied.

Having had occasion to make use of these bulletins, I undertook to solve the problem of authorship. It was necessary to show at the outset that all the bulletins examined were written by the same person. This was proved by cross references from one bulletin to another and by the appearance of similar expressions in two or more bulletins. The unity of the bulletins being established, search was instituted for matter indicating who the writer was. The following facts were established: (1) He was a member of the third estate; (2) he represented Barrois; (3) his bulletins were addressed to the people of Lorraine; (4) he was on very familiar terms with the deputies from Nancy; (5) he was a member of the Committee on Food Supply. What member of the assembly would those requirements fit? The Committee on Food Supply was made up of one representative from each of the generalities, or administrative divisions, into which France was divided. The list of this committee was found in the printed records of the assembly and opposite the generality of Lorraine was the name, Duquesnoy. An examination of the biography of Duquesnoy showed that he represented Barrois in Lorraine; that he had formerly lived at Briey in Barrois, which he represented as a member of the third estate, but that he had lived for some years previous to 1789 in Nancy, where he had been a man of prominence. He was naturally well acquainted with the representatives of Nancy in the assembly. The author of the bulletins was undoubtedly Duquesnoy.

To learn the name of the writer of a source it is often necessary to examine the entire source, and even then it is sometimes impossible to solve the problem. At other times, the solution is found within the compass of a few pages. If the author of Bailly's *Mémoires* was not known, it could be determined by reading the few pages of the *Mémoires* included in "The Oath of the Tennis Court," one of my *Source Studies on the French Revolution*. On the day of "The Oath of the Tennis Court," June 20, 1789, the writer of the *Mémoires* represents himself as receiving letters from the master of ceremonies notifying him that there would be no session of the

assembly on that day. He replied that on the day before he had adjourned the assembly until the morning of the twentieth, and it would be necessary for
it to meet. We infer from this that he was the pre-
siding officer of the assembly. After replying to the
master of ceremonies, the writer states that he called
together the secretaries of the assembly and that
they decided the session must be held. He went with
them to the hall and, although refused admittance,
declared the assembly in session. Later in the day he
opened and presided over the session in the tennis
court, where, as he wrote, "I asked on account of
my rank as president, to take the oath first." All of
this information is found in nine pages. Bailly's
name is not mentioned, but it is clear that the writer
was president of the assembly on June 20, 1789.
What was his name? In the same collection of
sources are the minutes of the assembly for June 20,
signed by "Bailly, President." Knowing now who the
writer was, there is no difficulty in gathering information in regard to him.

In a study on "The Royal Session of June 23,
1789," also one of the *Source Studies on the French
Revolution,* is an unsigned letter written from Paris,
June 29, 1789. Who was the writer? The original
is in Italian. The letter opens with the sentence,
"Tuesday, the 23d of the present month, was a very
interesting day as I have informed the Most Excellent Senate in my respectful communication." Here
is enough material to enable us to solve the problem.

[65]

The letter was clearly written in France, by an Italian ambassador, to a government with a senate at its head. What government in Italy was governed by a senate in 1789? Only one, Venice. The letter was written, then, by the Venetian ambassador. Who was the Venetian ambassador to the French court in 1789? The records in the Venetian archives would answer that question: his name was Antonio Capello.

To know what kind of man the witness was is the main object of the efforts of the critic, for upon the character of the witness depends the value of his testimony. Knowledge of the writer's name is of no particular value, if, after the name is known, it reveals nothing further about the man. To know that a certain unsigned letter was written by Jefferson is valuable information, for we know who Jefferson was and can make use of our knowledge of his character in estimating the value of what he wrote. But to know that another unsigned letter was written by John Smith is not at all valuable, if John Smith is an unknown person. This consideration raises the further question as to how we can evaluate the testimony of a witness who is known to us only through the written record he has left us. This problem differs only in kind from the one we have been dealing with. Instead of learning the name of the writer and then obtaining information about his personality from other sources, we are unable to learn his name, or his name does not help us, and we are forced to base our judgment of the man upon what he has written. The question runs, then, "What kind of a-man would write a letter or a book like this?" Reading between the lines, we make note of everything that may help us to form an opinion touching his natural ability, his education, his position in life, his opportunity to observe what he has described, his prejudices, his honesty and his ability to describe what he has seen.

From a letter in my *Studies,* written June 24, 1789, take the following extracts as an example of what may be learned from a short letter concerning the personality of the writer: "I passed Monday and Tuesday at Versailles. Monday it was announced to us on our arrival, that the royal session was adjourned. It rained. Guards prevented the deputies from entering the hall. It was a frightful spectacle for the good citizens to see our worthy representatives running in the streets without knowing where to assemble. The Recollets had the shamelessness to refuse their church. The curé of Saint-Louis offered his. There I was the witness of the most beautiful spectacle that I have seen in my life, the union of 149 deputies of the clergy. . . . The next morning Versailles was overrun by the crowd of strangers gathered for the session. The Archbishop of Paris and the guard of the seals were hooted at, derided, spit upon and so abused that they would have perished from rage and shame, if they had had any spirit. . . . The king came. As M. Necker did not precede him, we were in consternation. A handful of

paid children ran beside the carriage crying: Long
live the king. Some valets, some spies joined the
chorus; all the respectable people and the crowd kept
silent. . . . The third estate remained assembled
until three o'clock. . . . M. de Brézé came to tell
them to separate. 'The king,' said Mirabeau, 'can
have our throats cut; tell him we are awaiting death;
but he cannot hope to separate us until we have made
a constitution.' . . . In a word, all showed a Roman
firmness and decided to seal our liberties with their
blood. All Paris is in an uproar; the Palais-Royal is
as full as an egg; the Duc d'Orleans is rapturously
applauded everywhere."

What kind of a man wrote this letter? Clearly an
educated man, for he writes exceedingly well. He is
evidently young, for he is full of enthusiasm, impul-
sive in his utterances, interested in what is going on,
physically able to be about in Paris and Versailles,
mingling with the crowd in foul weather as well as
in fair. He was an eyewitness to such of the events
of June 23 as could be seen by the active man-in-the-
street. Not being a member of the assembly, he knew
about what went on in the hall only through hearsay.
He is a radical, an enthusiastic supporter of the third
estate and the revolution and, for these reasons, not
an unbiased observer. He does not question very
critically the information that comes to him—as for
instance, the two appearances of Brézé, a thing that
did not take place and concerning which he might
easily have informed himself—nor does he weigh his

words in describing what he has seen or what has been reported to him. These things render his report inaccurate and untrustworthy. In reading it, we feel that we have before us the statement of a partisan and not of a fair-minded, unprejudiced witness. All this, and it is much, we can learn from the reading of the letter. The knowledge that the letter was written by Camille Desmoulins will not lead to any serious modification of the portrait we have sketched.

Acquaintance with the character of the source—letter, newspaper, memoir, etc.—and with the personality of the writer does not offer a complete basis for the evaluation of a written tradition. The character of the source may be satisfactory. It may be a private letter, for example, and the witness may be intelligent, well informed, willing and able to tell the truth, and yet the record may not be satisfactory because of the space of time intervening between the occurrence of the event and the making of the record. The longer the interval of time, the more untrustworthy the record; it is a problem in memory. The more remote the event described by a witness, the less he can remember about it and the more uncertain he is as to the truth of what he can recall. A witness wholly dependent upon his memory never knows when he is telling the truth, no matter how honestly he may try to do so. To take an oath that one will tell the truth is equal to attempting to lift one's self by one's own bootstraps.

The memory has been experimented with in the

laboratory. A person is allowed to inspect a picture and the following day, without having seen the picture again, is requested to describe it and to underscore everything he feels certain about, everything he would be willing to swear to in court. Such a record is made several times, at intervals of a few days, the witness writing what he can recall about the picture and underscoring what he is certain about. A comparison of these different records shows two things: (1) The record grows steadily more untrustworthy, but (2) the certainty of the witness concerning the truth of certain things does not decrease.

The significant point for the historian is that the things about which the witness is confident are, for the most part, untrue. Other experiments have explained this curious phenomenon. The images which pass through the brain in the attempt to recall the past are composed of genuine recollections of past experiences and pure creations of the imagination. The genuine recall is hazy and incomplete, while the purely imaginative images are clear and detailed. The fact that a witness affirms that he can recall clearly some incident that happened months or years before does not prove the truth of what he recalls. From these experiments, at least one thing is clear, namely, the longer the witness delays committing his recollections to paper, the less valuable they are. The time of writing is, then, a very important matter.

When a source is not dated, or the writer does not state when he wrote his recollections, how can we fix the date? The problem is solved, generally from a study of the text, by fixing two *termini:* the *terminus post quem* and the *terminus ante quem,* the *date after which* and the *date before which* the account was written. To do this, a considerable knowledge of the history of the period in which the witness lived is necessary. The work must have been written after the date of the last event mentioned in the book and before the death of the writer. To fix the *terminus post quem* we read the text carefully, noting the dates of the events mentioned; the latest date is the terminus. But to fix only the *terminus post quem* is not sufficiently exact. The account was clearly written after a certain date, say 1789, but how much later? Perhaps the writer did not die until 1815, and we have a leeway of twenty-six years. Something must be done to eliminate a part of this long stretch of time, to draw the *terminus ante quem* nearer to the *terminus post quem.*

As the one limit is fixed by what the writer knows, the other is determined by what he apparently does not know. Suppose, for example, the last event mentioned in the source took place in the spring of 1789, and suppose that the work was written by a distinguished French nobleman, a man much attached to the old institutions, who afterward, in the summer of 1789, emigrated. Suppose furthermore that in dealing with the events of the revolution up to June, 1789, no mention is made of the action of the third estate on June 17, when it declared itself the national assembly, of the "Oath of the Tennis Court" of June 20, of the "Royal Session" of June 23, or of the great uprising of July, 1789, and the fall of the Bastille. Supposing all these things, is it likely that the work was written after June, 1789? Is it likely, if the book had been written after these events and by such a man, that he would not have referred to them in some way? It is very unlikely.

To fix the date of a letter may be easier than to determine when a witness wrote his memoir or recollections. Take, for example, the letter of Camille Desmoulins, already quoted. Suppose it were not dated, would it be possible to fix the date from the contents of the letter? Near the close of the letter Desmoulins writes: "M. Necker gave his resignation; all the deputies went *yesterday evening* to say farewell." As it is a well-known fact that the deputies called on Necker on the evening of June 23, it is clear that Desmoulins wrote his letter the next day, June 24, probably in the morning, as he does not mention the fact that the majority of the clergy joined the third estate on that day.

If the letter of the Venetian ambassador were not dated, it would be possible to date it very closely. The events described are those of June, 1789. The last event mentioned is "the union of the three orders in the hall of the states general," which took place on June 27. Hence the letter must have been written shortly after this, before anything else of importance had taken place. After the union of June

27, the assembly did not meet again until June 30. The inference would be that if Capello had written his letter after the thirtieth, he would have said something about this first meeting, a very important one. We should fix the date then as either June 28 or 29. The date shows that the letter was written on the twenty-ninth.

A letter by the Swedish ambassador at the French court, found in the same collection with the letters of Desmoulins and Capello, could, if not dated, have its date fixed definitely. "The majority of the clergy," runs the text, "went to the national assembly yesterday, and this morning forty-seven noblemen." It is well known that these things happened on June 24 and 25: the letter must have been written on June 25.

Another illustration from the same collection is the letter of Biauzat, a member of the third estate in the national assembly of 1789. Writing to his constituents about the royal session he said, "One of the last expressions of the king was for us to meet *tomorrow* in separate chambers." The letter was written on June 23, the day of the royal session.

The collection of the letters of Marie Antoinette by La Rocheterie and Beaucourt contains an example of an unsuccessful attempt to date an undated letter. The letter is addressed to the Comte de Mercy, the Austrian ambassador at the French court. The editors assign the letter to July, 1789. It was clearly written after October 6, 1789, as the queen refers to the intention of the king to recall his bodyguards and the opposition of the people of Paris to this act. This reference would have no meaning until after the invasion of Versailles in October, 1789, and the dissolution of the guard.

The problem of determining the date of writing of a volume of recollections is solved in the same way as that of the date of a letter, but demands more time and does not always yield satisfactory results. One may sometimes read through hundreds of pages without finding anything as a basis for the *termini*. As a rule, however, enough is found to make it possible to determine whether the record was made at once or some years later. Not infrequently a journal, written at the time, may be changed before printing, or notes taken at the time of an event may be incorporated with little change in a narrative written several years later. One should be on one's guard and not attribute the whole work either to the earlier or the later period. Young's *Travels in France* is an example of the first kind of work; the *Mémoires* of the Marquis de Bouillé of the last.

The *Mémoires* of Bailly has the form of a diary and by some writers was supposed to have been written from day to day. The use of such expressions as "yesterday," "today," "this morning," etc., give support to the idea, but other expressions, such as "at that time," "since," "that same day," "I do not remember," and an opening sentence in which Bailly writes, referring to his experiences during the revolution, "reduced to my memory to retrace them at this moment in my mind, and to commit them to this journal, I protest that my memory will be faithful," make clear that the work was written some years after the events it describes.

When was the work written? It was begun after November 18, 1791, for in the opening pages of the first volume Bailly refers to the work as "the journal of my life for thirty-one months." From April, 1789, when he entered public life, to November 18, 1791, when he ceased to be mayor of Paris, was thirty-one months.

He probably did not begin to write until January, 1792, when he was settled at his country place near Nantes, for on page 358 of volume one, Bailly uses the expression, "today, February 23, 1792." All of the work from this point on was written after this date. The portion between pages 358 in volume one, and page 303 in volume two, was written before June 14, 1792, as on the latter page we find the expression, "up to the time at which I write (June 14, 1792)." The *Mémoires* breaks off abruptly at page 409 of this volume. The last hundred pages must have been written before the news of the insurrection of June 20, 1792, had reached Nantes, for, after hearing this news, Bailly travelled through the departments. The writing, interrupted at this time, was never taken up again. The writing of the *Mémoires* was evidently begun in January, 1792, and ended in July of the same year. As the work treats of the events happening between April and October, 1789, it was written nearly three years after the events had taken place. What effect this has on the value of Bailly's recollections I shall consider later.

The question, Where was the source written?—the third subproblem under localization—is closely related to the first two, although not, as a rule, as important in the evaluation of the source as the personality of the writer and the time of writing. When a record is not a source in the best sense, a record made by an eyewitness of what he has seen, but made by a contemporary who obtained his information second-hand, the place of writing becomes important. The question is, Was the writer in a position to obtain good second-hand evidence? Again, when the record is the account of an eyewitness, but not written at the time the event occurred, it is important to know whether, at the time of writing, he was at the place where the events took place and was able to refresh his memory from other sources. Sometimes the place of writing can be inferred by references made by the writer; often it has to be learned from outside information and from inference. For example, Bailly wrote his *Mémoires* in the spring of 1792; we know that he was at his country house near Nantes at this time; hence the *Mémoires* was written at that place.

An excellent illustration of how the place of writing may be inferred from the content of a source is given by Bernheim. In the early part of the nineteenth century, there were discovered in the monastery of Saint Michael in Lüneburg, a few sheets of parchment manuscript containing annals for the years 1057 to 1130. Neither the name of the author nor the time and place of writing was given. The part from 1100 on was clearly the work of a contemporary. Where was it written? The handwriting was of the twelfth century, but showed no local peculiarities. The same was true of the language, which was the Latin of the twelfth century. The place of discovery might point to lower Saxony as the region in which it was written, but not without further proof. An examination of the contents showed that the part from 1100 on bore the stamp of unity; it was written by one person evidently. Who was this person?

Saxon events are treated in great detail, while events taking place in the rest of Germany, even when important, are simply mentioned or not referred to at all. Changes in the bishops of different bishoprics occupy much space, and the author is especially interested in the bishoprics of Magdeburg, Bremen, Halberstadt and Merseburg, Saxon bishoprics. Most of the princes whose deaths are mentioned are Saxon, and the writer assumes that when he refers simply to "Markgraf Rudolf" or to "Graf Friedrich," the reader will understand him. The deaths in the family of the counts of Stade are given regularly and the writer assumes the reader is acquainted with these relatively unimportant lords. "Udo comes," "Count Udo," is the regular form of reference. So great is the interest in this family that in the midst of the account of the struggle between Henry IV and his son, the annalist breaks off his narrative to note that "Count Linderus with the surname of Udo was taken sick, was brought to the monastery of Rosenfeld and died there." The mention of this monastery in connection with the Count of Stade is an important clue. Investigation shows that the monastery of Rosenfeld is located on the land of the Count of Stade, that it was founded by the counts of Stade.

Who, then, would be as much interested in the counts of Stade as a monk in the monastery of Rosenfeld, who wrote his annals for the circle of readers around him? And a notice from the year 1130 points unmistakably to the monastery of Rosenfeld as the place where the annals were written. "Cono abbas obiit," "the Abbot Kuno died," runs the record. Only in the monastery in which the annals were written could a reference like that—a reference that did not give the name of the monastery over which Kuno presided—be understood. From other sources we learn that Kuno was the abbot at the head of the monastery until 1130. It was here, clearly, that the annals were written.

The localization of the sources does not constitute the whole of criticism. The object of criticism is to discover the relation of the witness to the fact, to what really took place. We have assumed, up to this point, that the record contains nothing but what the witness actually saw or heard. That is seldom true and before we go farther we must analyze the source to determine definitely how much of it is first-hand and how much second-hand material. That being settled, it remains to determine, if possible, where the second-hand material came from. Sometimes the witness states himself that he saw or heard certain things, but not infrequently the knowledge that what he has recorded is first-hand material is a matter of inference. We know that he was present or was not present in a certain place at a certain time and that he could or could not have seen and heard these things.

Camille Desmoulins, for example, tells what Mirabeau said to Brézé in the hall of the estates on June 23. We know that the session was not open to the public on that day and that Desmoulins was not a deputy; hence he could not have heard the apostrophe of Mirabeau to the master of ceremonies. We infer that he saw the king arrive from the way in which he refers to it and to the cries that were raised.

When a deputy who was present in the hall tells what took place there, it is probably first-hand evidence, but when he tells us what took place outside while he was inside, we infer that the matter is second-hand.

When Necker tells us in his memoir that the king was probably called out of a council meeting on June 19, 1789, by order of the queen, we infer it is not first-hand evidence, but inference. He could not have seen the queen send the messenger, he did not hear what the messenger said and he did not see what took place after the king left the council chamber.

With the knowledge of who the witness was, where he was at a given time, what he could have seen and what he could not have seen, as a touchstone, we go through his narrative separating what he saw and heard from what he learned from others. The first part we can then evaluate on the basis of the character of the source, the personality of the writer and the time and place of writing.

The evaluation of the source is the goal toward which all our criticism up to this point has been moving. Is the source of such a *character,* has the witness such a *personality,* was the record made at such a *time* and in such a *place* that we can place a high degree of confidence in the affirmations found in the source? If the source is a private letter, written by an intelligent, well-informed and honest person, at the time and in the place where the event took place, we say it has the highest possible value. If the form is a public pamphlet, written by an individual of limited intelligence, low morality and little opportunity to inform himself, written long after the events and not in the place at which the events occurred, we place the lowest value upon it. Between these two lie all possible kinds of combinations, one or more of the elements possessing a low degree of value.

For example, the source might be a letter written by an able, well-informed and trustworthy person, but might treat of events which happened long before the date of writing; or the character of the source may be satisfactory and all the other elements—personality of the writer, time and place—unsatisfactory.

The evaluation, under the most favorable conditions, does not possess mathematical accuracy. After studying the source, we reach the conclusion that the affirmations of the witness *as a whole* possess little, much, or great value. Yet this is not the last word. While the evidence as a whole may be very valuable, certain portions, single affirmations, may possess little or no value. Consequently each affirmation must be judged on its own merits, must be carefully scrutinized, and no doubtful affirmations must be allowed to slip past us because the witness is trustworthy as a whole. On the other hand, in the testimony of a generally untrustworthy witness may be found some affirmations of the highest value that can not be rejected on the ground that the evidence as a whole is untrustworthy.

The close connection between the judgment passed upon the individual affirmation and the sum total of information derived from the previous criticism of a source should now be clear. We do not localize and analyze a source simply as a matter of form, and then forget what we have learned, but we are obliged to have the data at our fingers' ends and use it consciously, as we would use our knowledge of the personality of a witness if we were cross-examining him in the courtroom. We have in mind, at the same time, all the various kinds of errors the witness may commit and how many and what errors a witness such as we have before us would be likely to commit. The possibilities of error, between the time when the witness fixes his eye on the event and the moment when he writes down what he thought he saw, are many.

In the first place, to see or hear correctly what is going on, the witness must have normal senses. A man who is near-sighted, color-blind, hard of hearing or otherwise defective, might make a poor witness. Furthermore, the witness must possess enough natural intelligence to interpret correctly the signals which the senses are constantly sending in to the brain. And this interpretation calls not only for good normal mental powers, at least, but educated mental powers as well. It has been well said that "the eye sees in an object what the eye brings power of seeing." Other things being equal, an electrician will describe a new electrical machine more correctly than a common machinist; a theologian will reproduce the doctrinal arguments in a sermon more fully and exactly than a layman; a soldier will describe a battle better than a civilian.

The mind does not, however, reproduce all the senses present to it; it is obliged to choose. Here again a trained mind is necessary. Unless the important details are seized, the event cannot be correctly described.

After the details have been noted they must be grouped, organized to form a connected whole, an observation. Perhaps this is the most difficult task and the one performed with the least success by the ordinary mind.

The steps of sense impression, mental selection of details and grouping of details have been treated as if they took place in chronological order and formed a conscious operation. The truth is, of course, that all three operations are going on at the same time and for the most part unconsciously. In this respect, the material with which the historian works is much less valuable than the direct, conscious observations, many times repeated, of the natural scientist.

The impression once received, it remains to commit it to writing. Here a new possibility of error arises. Assuming that the witness has a clear, correct and well-organized observation in his mind, the problem is to express it so exactly in language as to convey to the mind of another ideas similar to those existing in his own. How few witnesses can do that! How few write consciously, how few are able to use words with the nicety imperatively necessary if a correct image and fine distinctions are to be conveyed from one mind to another! Not infrequently the reader is obliged to correct the account, helping the writer to say what he intended to say.

All these possible errors must be kept in mind and

the investigator must be on the alert for the errors to which each witness seems liable. To make the measure full, it must not be forgotten that prejudice, dishonesty, personal interest and party passion are constantly at work distorting the impression received by the witness. Along with them works time, blotting from the mind details and outline until the correct impression entirely disappears. There is no space here to illustrate the various ways in which these influences work in lessening the value of testimony. One class of sources, however, must be especially mentioned, the memoirs.

Historians of the last generation made large use of memoirs and the uncritical use of them is still common. Of all kinds of written tradition in which the witness is honestly endeavoring to tell the truth, probably no kind is less trustworthy than this. The cause of the untrustworthiness is to be found in forgetfulness due to the length of time that has elapsed between the observation of the event and the writing down of the record.

The material found in memoirs falls into two principal classes: (1) Affirmations touching matters of fact and (2) opinions and judgments of the witness upon what he has experienced. The one is of no more value than the other. As a rule, such affirmations in memoirs as we are able to check up by other evidence prove so untrustworthy that we hesitate to make use of those we cannot control. The writer himself, if an educated man, realizes that his memory is untrustworthy and attempts to supplement it by utilizing other source material, such as documents, letters, newspapers, etc., in which the event was recorded at the time it took place. This material is sometimes incorporated bodily into the text, sometimes reproduced in substance. What value is added to the affirmation of witness in a letter written in 1789, if we find it reproduced in the same language—evidently copied from the letter—in memoirs written by the same witness in 1804? Not the same value certainly as if the fact were recalled independently of the letter. But even in that case—the repetition of the same statement in substantially the same form by the same witness—could we be sure that the witness was telling the truth? A witness could certainly recall a false impression, without knowing that it was false.

When the writer of memoirs does not make use of other sources to refresh his memory and supply his narrative with details, the narrative is generally superficial, lacking in detail and objectivity. The reason Bailly's *Mémoires* is so full of detail is that he trusted very little to his memory, building up his narrative from the minutes of the assembly and of the city government of Paris, from letters, newspapers and documents, much as the modern historian would do. I have examined the two volumes of his *Mémoires,* comparing the text with the text of the sources he used, and was able to find the sources for nine-tenths of what the *Mémoires* contained; the amount of pure recollection is very small. In establishing the facts of the French revolution, the scientific historian should never think of quoting the text of Bailly when the text is only the literal reproduction of the *Point du jour,* the *Courrier de Provence* or the *Procès-verbal* of the assembly; he should go directly to these sources.

But Bailly describes the events in which he took a prominent part, and when he reproduces the account given in a source written at that time, is not that equivalent to saying, "This is the way I remember it"? If so, how much nearer certainty does the repetition of the first source bring us? The problem is, perhaps, unanswerable. Sometimes the statement reproduced may be correct and at other times incorrect. If we have only the single original source and the reproduction, how can we tell whether the original is correct or not, and if we do not know that, how can we tell whether the repetition is correct or not? In a word, when we can check up the source written at the time by another independent source written at the time, we are not helped by the repetition of the first source in memoirs written several years later.

The opinions and judgments of a witness found in his memoirs, purporting to be what he felt and thought at the time of the events, are no more valuable than his affirmations touching the events themselves, for they are equally subject to lapses of memory. Opinions and judgments of a witness concerning what he has seen or heard are valuable if they were recorded at the time the events took place. Contemporary letters and diaries are full of such matter, and very valuable matter it is, but it has little in common with a record of these same impressions as seen through the haze of years.

The *Mémoires* of Madame Roland, written on the eve of her execution and containing a sketch of her early life, conveys a quite different conception of her early sentiments and ideals from that obtained from letters written during her girlhood; in her *Mémoires,* she had read into her earlier life the sentiments and ideals of her later life.

The opinions and judgments expressed in memoirs have value, to be sure, if we wish to know the point of view of the writer at the time the memoirs were written, but as a rule such matter is of less interest than the opinions of the witness, recorded on the spot, concerning great events in which he may have participated. The final word concerning memoirs as evidence would seem to be that they should be used when no better sources can be found, but used with an understanding that a synthesis based upon them is of very uncertain value.

V

CRITICISM OF THE SOURCES: INDEPENDENCE

Up to this point, we have had under consideration only the first-hand material contained in a source. What shall be done with the second-hand material we have encountered? It is necessary to know from what source this information is drawn, that, if possible, we may use the record of the original witness instead of the second-hand reproduction. If the original cannot be found, the reproduction may be used, with certain reservations to be considered later in connection with the establishment of the fact. Here we wish to consider the problem of the dependence of the sources, of which the question of the origin of a second-hand account is only a part.

It frequently happens, in reading and criticising the sources dealing with an event, that we are struck by the fact that the same incident is related in two or more sources with the same details, arranged in the same order and reported in the same or nearly the same language. Such resemblance does not indicate that the facts reported are true, but that the sources reporting it have borrowed from each other or from a source to us unknown. The basis for the assumption is the psychological truth that no two *independent witnesses can report the same detailed event, giving the same details, in the same order and in the same language.* When such resemblance is noted, in reading the sources, we have a problem in dependence. How is it solved?

The first question is, Is one of the sources the original and the other the borrower? We may have already sufficient information about the two sources to enable us to answer that question. If, for example, in comparing the *Mémoires* of Bailly with the *Procès-verbal* of the national assembly for the events of June 23, 1789, we find the two recording the vote of the assembly on the decrees in almost the same language, Bailly saying, "These two votes were taken in the presence of several members of the clergy. Those whose credentials had been verified, gave their opinions at this time; the others asked that mention be made of their presence," and the *Procès-verbal,* "These votes were taken in the presence of several members of the clergy. Those whose credentials had been verified gave their vote at the same time with their opinions; the others asked that mention be made of their presence," it is clear there is dependence. The *Procès-verbal* was written at the time, Bailly's *Mémoires* three years later; hence the *Procès-verbal* was probably copied by Bailly. The discovery of other passages common to both and even references in the *Mémoires* to the

Procès-verbal by title furnish convincing proof that Bailly drew material from this source.

A more difficult case of dependence is that of the *Point du jour* and the *Procès-verbal* for June 20, 1789. A large amount of material is found in the same form in both and yet both were written and published at the time of the events. Both were the work of eyewitnesses, one being written by the secretary of the assembly, Camus, the other by Barère, a member of the assembly. Localization shows that the *Procès-verbal* was published on June 21, while the *Point du jour* did not appear until the next day. Barère evidently used the printed *Procès-verbal* of June 21 to prepare his paper, which appeared on June 22. One or two incidents, not reported in the *Procès-verbal,* are recorded in the *Point du jour* by Barère from his own direct observation.

This same session of the assembly is also described in the *Mémoires* of Bailly, where material is found common to the *Procès-verbal* and to the *Point du jour.* That Bailly used the *Procès-verbal* we already know; that he was also dependent upon the *Point du jour* is shown by the content and form of the two accounts and by a direct reference to the title, *Point du jour,* in the *Mémoires.* Here are three sources in the exact sense of the term, records made by eyewitnesses of events they had seen, two of the records being printed within two days of the event, and yet the agreement of their affirmations does not give us certainty concerning the event recorded. Two of the witnesses, instead of recording what they remembered, copied the account of a third. Thus, instead of three independent accounts, we have one account by an eyewitness copied by two other eyewitnesses.

Much of the work of the older historians of the French revolution has been vitiated by the use of sources the relationship of which has not been determined. An examination of a group of these sources will make clear how dangerous such a practice is. Two newspapers, the *Moniteur* and the *Journal des débats,* and a contemporary history, *Histoire de la révolution française par deux amis de la liberté,* constitute a group of sources much used by the historians of the last generation, as a rule, without any critical study.

Let us first consider the relation of the *Journal des débats* to the *Moniteur.* If the topic selected for study is the abolition of the remnants of feudalism by the French national assembly on the famous night of August 4, 1789, we find material for this study both in the *Journal* and the *Moniteur.* It is true the material, or a large part of it, is literally the same in both papers, but a little matter of that kind did not trouble the uncritical historian. Here was the same fact stated twice in the same terms by two contemporary newspapers; that should be enough to prove it was true. For the critical historian it is just enough to render him suspicious. "Why are the two accounts almost literally the same?" he asks and thus sets the critical machinery in motion.

Here, evidently, are two related sources. What relationship exists between them? Is either a first-hand record, made at the time the event took place? It has already been stated, in connection with the forgery of the third volume of Bailly's *Mémoires,* that the publication of the *Moniteur* did not begin until November 24, 1789, and the part dealing with the events from May to November 24, 1789, was not compiled until several years later. It could not, then, have been a source for the events of August 4, 1789. Before asking where the material came from for the composition of the earlier part, let us note an important fact in the history of the *Journal des débats.* Although the file of the *Journal* found in the libraries begins in June, 1789, a critical examination of the paper shows that the publication did not begin until the latter part of August, 1789, and the preceding numbers were compiled in 1790.

Neither the *Moniteur* nor the *Journal des débats,* then, was in existence at the time of the debates of August 4, 1789, and both accounts found in the files of these papers are later reconstructions, although the reconstructions of contemporaries. How was the reconstruction accomplished and what is the relation of the reconstruction in the *Moniteur* to the reconstruction in the *Journal?*

It should be kept in mind that when the editors of the *Moniteur* prepared their back numbers for 1789, the reconstruction of the *Journal* for June, July and August, 1789, was in existence and might have been used. A comparison of the text of the *Moniteur* with that of the *Journal* shows that there are some passages in the *Moniteur* not found in the *Journal*. This suggests the possibility that the editors of the *Moniteur,* instead of copying the *Journal,* used the same sources that had been used by the editors of the *Journal.* How can that point be settled? By finding the sources used in the construction of the back numbers of the *Journal.*

That seems like hunting for a needle in a haystack, but it is not so difficult as it seems. Suppose— we ask ourselves—we had been among the editors of the *Journal* in 1790, and had been required to construct an account of the debate of the night of August 4, 1789, what source material could we have found and what would we naturally have used? It is highly probable that we would have used printed material. The printed material, then accessible, consisted of the *Procès-verbal,* or minutes of the assembly, and newspapers, among which the most prominent were the *Point du jour* and the *Assemblée nationale.* A comparison of the text of the *Journal* with the text of these three sources shows that, with the exception of one short extract, the whole account of the *Journal* can be found in their pages. In fact, it is almost wholly a compilation from the *Procès* and the *Point du jour.* Much of it was reproduced literally, some of it slightly modified in form, some changes of expression being necessary to make the extracts read continuously and to give to them the appearance of unity.

There is nothing technical or difficult about this comparison of texts. The volumes are placed side by side on the table, where the eye can readily pass from one to the other. We read the first incident of the session recorded in the *Journal;* the same incident is related in the *Procès-verbal* in the same language; the next incident is taken literally from the *Point du jour* with a slight change; the third from the *Procès,* with no change; the fourth comes literally from the *Point du jour,* while the account of the rest of the session, with the exception of six incidents, is composed of material from the *Point du jour* and the *Procès-verbal,* for the most part reproduced literally.

Of what value is the account in the *Journal des débats* for the study of the night of August 4? None whatever, apart from a scrap of source material found in its columns and not found in the sources with which we have compared it. This scrap itself must have come from some other source, probably from some other newspaper. Making a note of that single paragraph for future use, we discard the rest of the account.

Passing to the second problem, let us see what the relation of the *Moniteur* is to the *Journal des débats* and the sources used in its compilation. The account of the debates of the night of August 4, contained in the *Journal,* composed of the material in the *Procès-*

verbal and the *Point du jour,* was the most complete account accessible to the editors of the back numbers of the *Moniteur* when they began their work. They probably did not know the history of the *Journal* and made no distinction between the reconstructed part and the genuine newspaper. The account in the *Journal* is in the third person, and no attempt is made to give to it the appearance of a parliamentary record. The *Moniteur* had been printing its accounts in this latter form and in making use of the text of the *Journal* it changed it to make it appear like a stenographic record, the name of each speaker being followed by his speech in the first person. A comparison of this text with the text of the *Journal* shows that the editors arbitrarily changed the person from third to first and made other changes in the text of the *Journal* to give the speech the appearance of an exact quotation. This makes the text of the *Moniteur* less valuable as a copy than that of the *Journal.*

In addition to the *Journal,* from which the great bulk of the material was drawn, the editors of the *Moniteur* made some use of two other newspapers, the *Courrier de Provence* and the *Assemblée nationale,* taking from them notices of incidents not mentioned in the *Journal.* But how do we know that the *Moniteur* took the most of its material from the *Journal* and not directly from the sources used by the *Journal?* Because (1) the same modifications in the text of the original sources made by the editors of the *Journal* also appear in the text of the *Moni-*

teur and (2) the same extracts arranged in the same order are found in both. No two persons, working independently, would make the same selections from two newspapers, arrange them in the same way and make the same changes in the language of the original; hence the material in the *Moniteur* was drawn from the *Journal*.

The material in the *Moniteur*, literally the same, or very nearly the same, as that in the *Assemblée nationale* or the *Courrier de Provence*, was evidently taken directly from these papers.

The *Moniteur*, then, is a compilation of three newspapers, and the newspapers of which the principal use is made is nothing but a compilation itself. The *Moniteur* is less valuable than the *Journal* as a copy and neither has any value as a source.

The third source to which reference has been made, the *Histoire de la révolution par deux amis de la liberté*, is related to the *Moniteur*, having been used by the editors of the *Moniteur* in its reconstructed numbers, but not for the account of the session of August 4, as Ranke erroneously believed. The first two volumes of the work were in print in July, 1790. Much has been written about the authorship of these volumes. It is commonly asserted, without any proof, that they were written by Kerverseau and Clavelin, but the authorship is of little importance, as the work is only a compilation. The account of the session of August 4 is woven together from fragments of the *Procès-verbal* and the *Cour-*

rier de Provence, the bulk of it being taken literally from the *Procès-verbal,* without quotation marks. This dependence is established (1) by reading the texts and noting that they are the same, (2) by showing that as the *Histoire* was not composed until after the *Procès-verbal* and the *Courrier de Provence* had been printed it must be dependent upon them.

What is true of August 4, is also true of other portions of the *Histoire* for 1789 that I have had occasion to examine; they are pieced together from sources still in existence. Flammermont, in his monograph on "July 14, 1789," says of the *Histoire* as a source for that period: "They make use especially of the *Procès-verbal des électeurs,* of the *Bastille dévoilée,* and of the *Prècis exact du Cousin Jacques.* . . . But they have no definite system; they have not made a critical study of any of the sources they have employed; they have confined themselves to choosing, upon any point, the version which appeared the most trustworthy to them; they have fallen into some of the strangest contradictions. . . . In short, the work has no original value." It has been used by historians for the uprising of October 5 and 6, 1789, and yet the editors state themselves that they made use of the depositions taken in 1789 and 1790 by the *Châtelet,* the criminal court of Paris, and accessible today in the published *Procédure criminelle.*

Dependence is often a very subtile thing. A good

illustration of this is found in connection with the events of June 22, 1789. On that day, it is said,—and this tradition is repeated in many of the histories of the revolution,—the national assembly did not meet in the tennis court, as it had done on June 20, because the Comte d'Artois had notified the owner of the court that he wished to play tennis that day, the real motive for his action being to prevent the meeting of the assembly. This story is found in the works of Thibaudeau and Dubois-Crancé, both members of the third estate and present in Versailles on that day. Neither man could have seen the narrative of the other, as both were published after the death of the writers. Here is apparent independence and seemingly the evidence should be sufficient to establish the fact.

But let us examine the problem a little closer. What was the date of writing of the two works? Thibaudeau's volume was written in 1804, Dubois-Crancé's in 1799, that is many years after the event. This made it possible for the two writers to hear and report the same tradition, which had become current and well fixed at the time when they wrote. Furthermore, they had no first-hand knowledge of the pretended message of the Comte d'Artois to the owner of the tennis court and it is doubtful if they could have had any other authority than hearsay for what they reported. Finally, there is an abundance of first-hand evidence to show that the tennis court was not reserved on that day for the Comte d'Artois, that a large number of people gained entrance to it and among them some of the members of the assembly. The meeting was not held there (1) because of the crowd, (2) because there were no seats or furniture of any kind, and (3) because a dignified meeting place was desired for that day, as the majority of the clergy was planning to join the assembly.

This example illustrates the way in which the different steps of the historical method are related to each other. To prove the dependence of our two sources on rumor, it was necessary to emphasize the fact that the writers had no first-hand knowledge of what they reported; that is, we made use of the distinction already mentioned between what the writer knew directly and what he knew only by hearsay. It then remained for us to show that this tradition conflicted with facts established by reliable, independent witnesses.

Another illustration of the agreement of contemporaries concerning a tradition about which they had no first-hand knowledge, is the statement that the heads of the two bodyguards assassinated at Versailles on the morning of October 6 were carried to Paris on pikes and were under the eyes of the king and queen during the long and frightful journey of that October afternoon. The tradition was formed early. A member of the assembly, Duquesnoy, writing to his constituents on October 7, exclaimed, "Think of that carriage, preceded by the heads of the bodyguards!" The anecdote has made its way into almost all the histories, and yet it is not true. The fact is established beyond the possibility of a doubt that the heads were in Paris before the royal carriage had left Versailles. Contemporaries who reported were dependent on rumor, although seemingly independent.

Enough has been said, I think, to make clear the difficulty of establishing the independence of witnesses and also the necessity of doing so. Only on a foundation of facts established by the agreement of trustworthy, independent witnesses can a permanent, scientific exposition of man's historic past be constructed. To laboriously collect all the sources and submit each one to the tests that have been described for genuineness, authorship, time and place of writing, and finally to compare them with each other in order to determine whether or not they are independent is a task that consumes a vast amount of time and demands an equal amount of patient endeavor. In no other way, however, can history be scientifically written. The refusal to recognize this patent fact and, at the same time, to fail to distinguish between popular and scientific historical expositions, has made the work of the scientific historian needlessly laborious. When an historian has carefully studied the sources of the period upon which he is engaged, the practice has been to treat the results of his critical studies as so much waste product after they have aided him in the construction of a scientific narrative. It is an indefensible practice.

CRITICISM OF THE SOURCES

The same sources used for the construction of a study on one topic may be used later for the preparation of another topic taken from the same period. Why should the later investigator be obliged to repeat all the critical work accomplished by his predecessor and why should this work still remain unformulated and the labor of Sisyphus go on forever? If each one formulated and printed the results of his preliminary critical work, in determining, for example the authorship of the journal attributed to Duquesnoy, the genuineness of the third volume of Bailly's *Mémoires,* or the *Journal of a Spy,* the time when Bailly wrote his *Mémoires,* or the dependence of the *Moniteur* upon the *Journal des débats* and of both upon the *Procès-verbal* and the newspapers of the period, how much easier it would make the work of the historian of the early French revolution, and how much bad historical work would be prevented.

All investigators have not the patience to do the critical work themselves, but they are willing to profit by it when they find it ready to their hands. This by-product of the historian's labors should be preserved in an appendix, in footnotes, or published apart in an historical review. It matters little where and when it is made public, if it is only preserved.

The student of modern European history suffers more from the failure to publish critical studies than the worker in the ancient and mediaeval periods. There exists a false notion among historians of modern history to the effect that this preliminary critical work is something peculiar to the older fields of history; that work in modern history is immune from it, that it is unnecessary there. It has even been asserted that ancient and mediaeval history offer better opportunities than modern history for training in critical study. The correct statement of the case would be that more critical study has been done in ancient and mediaeval history, that in those periods it is regarded as indispensable and a student specializing in mediaeval history under well-trained instructors is more likely to be critically trained than one specializing in modern history.

No historian ever published more varied critical work of a high quality than Leopold von Ranke, the great German historian of the last century and probably the greatest of all historians. The productive period of his life was of extraordinary length, his first work being published when he was twenty-nine years of age, his last sixty years later. His first volume contained a critical supplement in which he criticised the printed sources upon which the history of the period had hitherto been based. This practice was continued through all his later works even into his *Weltgeschichte*, written in the last six years of his life. In these *Analekten*, as he called them, can be found classical examples of the solution of most of the problems with which the historian has to deal. The young historian could find no better means of supplementing his theoretical study of method than by working over carefully these *Analekten* of Ranke.

VI

ESTABLISHMENT OF THE FACTS

THE aim of criticism is the evaluation of the sources and the determination of their relationship, but evaluation is not an end in itself; it is the indispensable preliminary to the establishment of the facts. The criticism of the sources does not give us the facts; it puts us in a position to compare critically the affirmations of the independent witnesses by means of which the facts are established. This distinction between an *affirmation* and a *fact* is of fundamental importance and should never be lost sight of. What one witness affirms that he saw or heard may or may not be the truth; if it is confirmed by the independent affirmation of another witness, we say it is a fact, or that it is certain that the thing is true. *As a rule, then, the condition of certainty is the existence of at least two independent witnesses to the same detailed fact.* If their affirmations agree, then the thing affirmed is a fact, unless the witnesses are self-deceived.

What is meant by this term self-deception? It is a psychic condition common to two or more witnesses which prevents them from interpreting correctly what they see or hear. For example, certain miracles of the Middle Ages are established by the agreement of the affirmations of two or more independent witnesses. Does this prove that the thing took place as the witness described it?

An illustration will make the point clear. Some years ago, I stood with a group of people in the midway of an exposition watching the manipulations of a sleight-of-hand performer. It was afternoon. The man stood upon a low platform, his flowing sleeves thrown back upon his arms, every condition seemingly unfavorable to the successful practice of visual deception. He held a tack between the thumb and forefinger of one hand and announced that he would insert it into the outer corner of his left eye. I watched him closely. He displayed the tack in his hand, raised the hand to the corner of his eye, seemingly pushed the tack in and then displayed the empty hand. The hand was again raised to the eye and the performer went through the process of pushing the tack across his forehead. Taking it out of the outer corner of the right eye, he displayed it to the crowd. He appeared to have accomplished what he had promised to do; his hands had worked so rapidly that the eye of the observer had not been able to detect the imposition.

Had this crowd been a gathering of mediaeval folk it would have reported a miracle and proved it by the agreement of a number of honest, independent witnesses. But no one in that gathering, it is safe to assume, believed that the tack had passed under the skin across the man's forehead, because they all knew enough about physiology to understand that the thing was impossible. They were not self-deceived; they knew that the eye was not able to report all that had taken place. The agreement of the two or more independent witnesses did not, then, establish the truth of the thing affirmed by the witnesses.

. It must be remembered that the foundation of the whole process of historical proof is possibility. If a thing is not possible, we cannot adduce sufficient historical proof to show that it was probable or certain. And what do we mean by a possibility? "A thing or event that *may* happen." To say that a thing is possible is in no way to assert that it *did* happen, that we have any *proof* that it happened, but simply to assert that there is nothing in the sum total of reliable human experience that would lead us to doubt the occurrence of such an event, *if sufficient trustworthy evidence existed to prove that it actually did take place.* If contemporary witnesses testified that they saw a certain old woman, supported only by a broomstick, flying over a chimney, we would dismiss the evidence summarily because we know that a broomstick is not a flying machine, and is incapable of supporting in the air and transporting through the air a body heavier than air. The thing is impossible. *The whole body of reliable human experience is against the possibility of the thing affirmed.*

It is affirmed in an historical document that on a

[105]

certain occasion water was changed into wine. The affirmation cannot be localized, that is, we do not know who saw this performance nor when he made a record of what he thought he saw, but even if the affirmation were of a more valuable nature, even if it could be definitely localized, it would not establish the probability of the thing asserted, *because all reliable human experience indicates that the thing could not have taken place.* We know what the chemical composition of wine is and what the chemical composition of water is and we know of no way in which the elements of water—oxygen and hydrogen—can be combined to produce wine, i.e., fermented grape juice. If the witness believed that he saw water changed into wine, he was self-deceived.

It should not be forgotten, however, that what was regarded as an impossibility in one age may become a possibility in another. At the same time it should be remembered that *the occurrence is shifted from the realm of impossibilities to that of possibilities only because fresh and more reliable human experience, exact and repeated experience, has shown that the thing may take place.*

One hundred years ago, if an individual had reported that he had seen a man flying in a machine heavier than air or that a message had been sent to Europe from America without the aid of wires, his testimony would have been dismissed without consideration on the ground of impossibility. Today these things have entered the realm of possibilities.

The fact that fresh human experience is constantly bringing what was regarded as impossible into the realm of the possible is of no assistance in dealing with affirmations touching the objects and events against the possibility of which all reliable human experience up to the present time has been arrayed. There may be possibilities among them, but only fresh scientific experiment can reveal them and until that comes these objects and events must be treated as impossible.

It should be noted that this fresh scientific experiment is contrasted with historical testimony, evidence dealing with a single occurrence. It is true that the first successful experiment is historical, a single event, but it must be repeated, it must become natural science, it must be rendered rationally intelligible before it can outweigh the accumulated past experience which asserted the thing to be impossible. Even the repeated experiments of a single scientist, which apparently change some scientific law, rendering possible what was before looked upon as impossible, are not regarded as valid until they have been repeatedly and carefully performed by other scientists and there is general agreement as to the results of the work.

On the other hand, we may not reason from possibility to probability. If a thing is not possible, it cannot be probable, but because it is possible it in no wise follows that it is probable. In the discussion of the probability of an event, it is not at all uncommon to hear the person whose statement is questioned exclaim, "But, is it not possible?" To his mind, possibility carried probability along with it.

To assert that a thing is possible is simply to affirm that, as far as human experience goes, there is nothing to indicate that the thing may not have taken place, but that is to say nothing as to whether the thing actually did take place at a certain time and in a certain way. *Evidence must be adduced to establish probability, or certainty, after possibility has been recognized.* Whether the evidence gives us a low or high degree of probability or whether it gives us certainty touching the occurrence, depends on the quantity and quality of the evidence. An event may be possible, but a single untrustworthy affirmation that it actually did occur may not move it from the background of possibility into the foreground of probability. A valuable single affirmation by an eyewitness may render the event highly probable, and the agreement of the affirmations of two independent witnesses may banish all doubt as to the truth of the matter.

These are the general conditions under which the historian works when he undertakes to establish the facts relating to some past event. What is the actual process he makes use of? Let it be noted, in the first place, that the truth of the complex whole he is seeking to restore is ascertained by determining the truth of the elements which are to constitute it. He must get his pieces of stained glass before he can put them together and form a rose window. He has acquired a conception of his whole subject by reading his sources for the purpose of criticising them. Time may be saved, when the process is understood, by interpreting the different sources at the very beginning of the work, even before the criticism has been undertaken.

Interpretation, in untechnical language, means reading over a source and making careful, detailed notes of the affirmations contained in the source relating to the subject under investigation. For this purpose a loose-leaved notebook may be used, the leaves having perpendicular red lines a short distance from the margins on the right and left sides of the sheet. The title of the source, with exact reference to edition, place and date of publication, the number of the volume from which the extracts are taken and the pages should be written at the top of the sheet. Between the red lines should be written the affirmations of the source; at the left, beyond the red line, should be given the page from which the affirmation was taken and at the right, beyond the red line, should be a side-head, to enable the student in running over the pages to note readily what they contain.

The card system of note taking—the cards being arranged in a box, each card with a heading and bearing a single affirmation—has some manifest advantages over the loose-leaved notebook. It is easier to run over the heads and see what one has, to at once put a fresh affirmation in the group with the older affirmations on the same point. The objection to the box of cards for the undergraduate is the inconvenience in handling it; the notebook is easier to carry about. For the advanced student, or the graduate who has a fixed place in a seminar room, this objection is not valid.

The notes taken by the historian in the interpretation of a source are of two kinds: general and detailed. For the first, a statement in his own language concerning the substance of the text may be sufficient. He wishes to know the date of a certain event. As he reads his sources, he looks for a statement touching this matter, and when he finds it, he is not concerned with the language of the text, but with the statement of the witness that the event happened on a certain day. But suppose the matter under investigation was the expression used by an historical character on a certain occasion. Then the language and the details become important and the historian should carefully copy the statement of each source in its original language.

It may be well to repeat here what has already been said about taking full and detailed notes upon sources that may not be accessible to the investigator when he begins his work of construction. These notes should not be translations and they should not be abridged. Whether the notes taken are general and condensed, or detailed and in the language of the text, will depend upon what the investigator is after and must be determined by him. The notes should be made carefully, condensations exactly representing the ideas in the source, reproductions of the text being literal and complete. Slovenly work here will render good work in the next stage impossible.

It should be realized at the outset that, in reading sources for scientific historical purposes, one must read more carefully than when engaged in gathering general information upon an historical period by the rapid reading of secondary works. *Accuracy is the first requisite in scentific work and only such speed is permissible as is compatible with accuracy. The chief desideratum in scientific work is to get the thing done correctly.* If it can be done correctly and at the same time rapidly, so much the better, but it must be done correctly even if it must be done slowly.

The sources having been interpreted and notes taken of the affirmations relating to the subject in hand, the next step is to determine one detail after another by bringing together and comparing all the affirmations relating to each detail. A practical way of doing this is to write at the top of a sheet the fact to be established and to copy under it all the affirmations relating to it, the affirmations being spaced, so that one can see at a glance how many there are, the work from which they are drawn being shown by bibliographical references at the left of the red line on the left-hand side of the sheet. In handling these affirmations, three kinds of problems arise: (1) We may have several independent affirmations and they may agree concerning the fact, thus giving us certainty; (2) there may be several independent affirmations and they may disagree, the result being either probability or suspended judgment, and (3) we may have only one affirmation.

The treatment of the first case is not difficult, if the critical work has been carefully done, that is, if we know that the affirmations came from first-hand, independent witnesses. Let us take as an example of the first problem an incident from the famous "Oath of the Tennis Court," of June 20, 1789. On the morning of that day, when the deputies reached their hall, they found it closed and guarded by troops, at least that is the statement of the secondary historians. This statement is made up of a number of details: (1) In the morning (2) of June 20, 1789, (3) the deputies of the third estate (4) went to their hall and (5) found it closed and (6) guarded by troops. Each of these details, if true, can be established by the agreement of the affirmations of independent witnesses.

On the last detail we have the affirmations of three independent witnesses, namely, (1) the minutes of the assembly,—*Procès-verbal,*—written by the secretary Camus, "The President and the two secretaries presented themselves at the principal entrance; they found it guarded by soldiers"; (2) the account in a daily paper,—*L'assemblée nationale,*— "Having arrived at the gate of the Menus (the hall), what a novel spectacle! The deputies found there French guards, officers of the guards, who with fixed bayonets and drawn swords would have plunged like vile assassins the sword of despotism into the breast of the citizen"; (3) a letter of Duquesnoy, a member of the third estate, "Yesterday, at the moment when the president presented himself at the assembly hall, he found it guarded by soldiers who refused him entrance." These affirmations are all by eyewitnesses, recorded at the time of the event and entirely independent of each other. They agree that the hall was guarded by troops. We are justified in stating this as a fact, without any reservation.

Notice that there are in the extracts other details not mentioned by all the witnesses. For instance, only one states that the troops were French Guards, only one gives the name of the hall, only one speaks of the presence of the secretaries, and only one refers to "fixed bayonets and drawn swords." All of these details would come under the third problem, where our knowledge rests upon the affirmation of a single witness and we get only probability.

As the statement that the president was attended by two secretaries was made by one of them, Camus, and recorded that day, shortly after the officers reached the hall, the probability that the affirmation corresponds to the fact is very high, as it is not a matter concerning which Camus could have been readily deceived or could have forgotten in so short a time.

The case for the French Guards is not so good. This statement is found in the newspaper written by Lehodey, a newspaper writer, but not a member of the assembly. He spent his time in Versailles, where the assembly was sitting, gathering news for his paper. He would have had opportunities enough to learn who the French Guards were, and as he was in the avenue before the hall on the morning of June 20, he would have had every opportunity to see the troops and recognize them as French Guards, although his affirmation to the effect that they were French Guards would not have the value of the affirmation of Camus, one of the secretaries, that the president was accompanied by the secretaries on the morning of June 20. Furthermore, Lehodey did not write his account of the events of the day until the day was over and had more opportunity to forget than Camus.

Let us turn now to the second and more difficult problem, where we have several independent affirmations, but they do not agree. I shall take as an illustration of this problem an example from the events of July 17, 1789. On that day, after the fall of the Bastille and the triumph of the revolution, Louis XVI visited Paris. As he was about to enter the city hall, Bailly, acting as mayor, presented him with a cockade, or rosette of ribbons. The historians say it was a tricolored cockade of red, blue and white. Is this true? The question is of no great importance, but every fact important enough to form a part of an

[114]

historical narrative is important enough to be stated correctly.

I have found one source in which it is affirmed that the cockade was tricolored. Duquesnoy, writing on the evening of July 17, said, "It is known that all the people of Paris wear a red, blue and white cockade . . . the king received one of them." Duquesnoy was with the king on that day, "almost always close to his carriage," so that he had every opportunity to see what was going on. This affirmation would seem to have as much value concerning the cockade as the affirmation of Lehodey would have touching the French Guards. If we had no other evidence, we should think it highly probable that the cockade worn by the king on July 17 was red, blue and white.

But let us look at the rest of the evidence. The *Procès-verbal* of the city government of Paris contains a decree passed on July 13, 1789, ordering all citizens enrolled in the militia "to wear a red and blue cockade." These were the colors of the city.

Gouverneur Morris, who sat in a window of the Rue St. Honoré and saw the king pass on July 17, wrote in his diary that day, "The king's Horse Guards, some of the Guards du Corps and all those who attend him, have the cockades of the city, viz. red and blue."

The Bailli de Virieu, the ambassador of Parma, who was in Paris at the time, wrote on July 20, "His Majesty came out of the city hall with a satisfied look and as soon as he appeared in the square with the red and blue cockade in his hat cries of 'Long live the king' were heard."

The Venetian ambassador, writing on July 20, refers to the cockade of the militia as "blue and red, the colors of the city," and in the same letters remarks that "it is proper for everybody without distinction to wear the cockade of the third estate which was changed from green to red, because the color green is that of the livery of the Comte d'Artois who has become the object of public hatred."

The *Procès-verbal* of the city government for July 17 says, "The king dismounted from his carriage at the entrance to the city hall and there M. Bailly presented to his majesty a cockade of the colors of the city" (that is, blue and red). This last affirmation would appear to be of great value, but unfortunately the *Procès-verbal* of July 17 was not written on July 17, as no minutes were kept at the time. The record as we have it was composed in the winter of 1789-1790 by a committee of the members of the city government who made use of notes taken at the time, of documents, and of statements made by members of the government, and their account when written was discussed by the city council and corrected. Whatever was left in the report represented what these men, all of them witnesses of the events of July 17, believed had happened. It was their opinion that the color of the cockade worn on that day by the king was blue and red, the colors of the city.

Camille Desmoulins, writing to his father on July 16 and referring to the visit of the delegation of the national assembly to Paris on July 15, spoke of "100,000 armed men and 800,000 with blue and red cockades."

On that day, evidently, all Paris was wearing the blue and red cockade. More evidence might be added to show that the cockade worn by Louis XVI on July 17 was not blue, red and white, but blue and red, the colors of the city of Paris. On the one side, we have the affirmation of Duquesnoy; on the other Morris, the Bailli de Virieu, the *Procès-verbal* and Camille Desmoulins, testifying either directly that the king wore a cockade of the city colors or that he wore the cockade everybody was wearing. The conclusion is that Duquesnoy was mistaken and that the king wore a red and blue cockade. These examples will serve to show how affirmations are treated in the establishment of a fact.

Thus far we have dealt only with the direct testimony of eyewitnesses, that is, with the most satisfactory kind of sources. For a large part of the history of Europe very little of this direct testimony exists. Compare our knowledge of the events of the French revolution with that of the history of the Greeks and Romans. Why do we know so much less about this earlier history and why is so much of our knowledge untrustworthy? The difference is due to the difference in the quantity and quality of the sources.

Take the statement that the Boeotians migrated from Thessaly to Boeotia before the Trojan war. It rests on the authority of Thucydides. When did the Trojan war take place, if there ever was a Trojan war? The traditional date is about 1000 B. C. Who was Thucydides, when did he live and write? He was an Athenian and lived and wrote about 400 B. C., that is, about six hundred years after the supposed migrations. How did Thucydides know anything about an event happening six hundred years before his day?

How do we know anything about what happened in 1300 A. D.? From the records of the time, but our knowledge of the events of 1300 is more reliable than the knowledge of Thucydides touching what happened six hundred years before his day, because in the fourteenth century men made written records of what happened; in the eleventh century B. C., they did not, nor for two centuries later.

For two hundred years, then, after the migration from Thessaly to central Greece—if it took place— the knowledge of the event must have been kept alive among an ignorant people solely by oral tradition. And what is an oral tradition worth that has circulated for two hundred years! Then it must have been written down and copied many times before it reached Thucydides at the end of six hundred years. Under these circumstances, does the affirmation of

Thucydides have any great value in establishing the fact of the migration?

Take any chapter of Holm's *History of Greece* and examine the footnotes given in support of the statements in the texts. Mark when the events took place, then note what the source is, who wrote it and when he wrote it. The amount of evidence that can be placed in the same class with that used above on the French revolution is practically nil. I am speaking, of course, of the testimony of eyewitnesses and not of documents. Herodotus is the chief source for the Persian wars, and, if he was alive at the time, he was an infant and could not have known anything about it personally. Plutarch is constantly cited as a source in Greek history and investigation will show that in the majority of cases the events he narrates occurred several hundred years before his own time and his information reached him after passing through many hands. Strabo is the chief source on Greek colonization, and yet he lived several hundred years after the colonies were founded. Even when the events are reported by a mature contemporary like Thucydides (the Peloponnesian war), Xenophon, or Polybius, still but a small part of what is reported by these historians could have been seen or heard by them personally.

Not all of our knowledge of any period rests upon the direct affirmations of eyewitnesses or the repetition of their reports by others. The historian also reaches conclusions touching what happened by means of inference, or constructive reasoning, as the process is called. The lawyer calls this kind of evidence circumstantial. An event takes place, something is done, but nobody but the actor witnessed it. From an examination of all the evidence we are led to the conclusion that it must have been done by a certain person.

A prominent citizen of Cambridge, Massachusetts, disappeared. He was last seen going into the laboratory of a professor of chemistry in Harvard College. The professor declared that he knew nothing of the man's whereabouts. It was known that the professor was the debtor of this gentleman and was finding it difficult to pay him. The janitor had noticed that the professor worked in his laboratory with locked doors. He examined the refuse from the professor's furnace and among other objects found teeth filled with gold. A local dentist recognized the teeth as belonging to the man who had disappeared. Other evidence was discovered indicating that the professor had cremated a human body in his laboratory and that the body was that of the missing man. The inference was that the professor had killed him. Later the professor confessed that the man had come to his laboratory, had demanded payment and that in a fit of anger he had struck and unintentionally killed him.

The records of the criminal courts are full of cases in which the guilt of the prosecuted persons can be established by circumstantial evidence alone.

In every case, our belief that the supposed criminal committed the deed is due to an *inference* from *facts established by direct testimony.* The value of this inference depends upon (1) the number of the facts established by direct testimony, (2) the closeness with which they fit together and (3) the improbability that any other fact than the fact established by inference could be fitted into the vacant space.

The work is not unlike the piecing together of a picture puzzle; when all the pieces are in place, one small hole has not been filled. What was the missing piece like? In some cases there can be no doubt. We were putting together a human figure, and perhaps a finger, an eye, or a button on the coat is missing. The problem is an easy one and our inference rises to the level of certainty. But there may be more than one piece missing, the holes to be filled in might be filled in different ways and one reconstruction might be as reasonable as another. There uncertainty begins and our inferences fall very low in the scale of probability.

Suppose we were standing with some person in the room of a house. We pass out of this room into another, leaving the person in the room, making our exit by the only door in the room. As we pass into the adjoining room, a man hurries past us with a knife in his hand and enters the room we have left. Immediately afterwards, we hear a cry and a fall, and, as we turn back, the stranger runs past us and escapes from the house. We enter the room and find lying on the floor the bleeding body of the person we had left there and by his side the knife—blood-stained—which we had seen in the hand of the stranger. We did not see the deed, but we infer that the murder was committed by the stranger. No one else was in the room, no one else could have entered the room. The knife in the hand of the stranger, the short interval that elapsed after he entered the room before the cry was heard, seem to leave room for no other inference than that he was the murderer.

But change the evidence a bit. Let there be two doors to the room; have two men in the room, seemingly in friendly conversation when we leave; allow a longer interval to elapse and add the sound of angry voices, heard from the room where we are, followed by a cry and fall. We enter the room and find a dead man stretched on the floor and the other man standing over him knife in hand. He tells us that a stranger did the deed and he simply drew the knife from the wound. No stranger can be found and the only plausible inference is that the one man killed the other as the result of a quarrel. There is, however, no evidence to show that the angry voices were the voices of these two men, and the possibility always remains that, as the defendant declares, some one else entered, quarrelled with and killed the other man in the presence of his friend.

The method of constructive reasoning may take on a negative character in the so-called "argument from silence." An individual who was well informed as to what took place at a certain place and within a certain time, writes about the events but does not mention a certain detail. It was a detail he would probably have known about and mentioned had it taken place; as he did not mention it, we infer it did not take place. There is much greater danger in this kind of reasoning than in positive inferences, because it is difficult to determine (1) whether the witness could have seen or heard the thing had it taken place and (2) whether he would certainly have recorded it had he seen it.

An excellent illustration of the danger lurking in this kind of reasoning is found in the royal session of June 23, 1789. It was in this session that Mirabeau made his famous reply to Brézé. Several independent witnesses, writing at the time, establish the certainty of the fact. The fact was an important one, must have been known, one would imagine, by every deputy in the hall and, had it been known, certainly would have been reported; and yet two of the deputies, Biauzat—in a letter to his constituents written that day—and Barère—in his newspaper, *Le point du jour,* written the same day—make no mention of the Mirabeau episode. If these two sources contained the only descriptions written by eyewitnesses of what took place on June 23 after the withdrawal of the king and if the accounts of Mirabeau's reply to Brézé were found only in contemporary works written by men who were not eyewitnesses, would we not be likely to say that in this case the argument from silence must be applied, that the Mirabeau incident never actually occurred?

Constructive reasoning should be employed only with the greatest caution, and the results stated in a scientific way, without any attempt to make them appear more probable than they really are. As training in exact work and as a means of control, it is well to arrange the inferences in logical form, thus making clear the fallacy in the argument, if there is one.

For instance, it is common in dealing with ancient history to infer that certain places in the Mediterranean were settled by Phoenicians because they bear Phoenician names. Let us put the argument into logical form. We note, as a matter of fact, the existence here and there of Phoenician names. This we are certain of. We have observed that it is a common practice for a people to give to a town a name taken from their own language. This we formulate in a major premise, "the names of towns are taken from the language of their founders"; as a minor premise, "the names of these towns are taken from the Phoenician language," hence "these towns were founded by Phoenicians." Upon what does the soundness of that conclusion rest? Upon two things, (1) the number and correctness of the facts forming the foundation for the minor premise and (2) the universal validity of the major premise. Is it true that the names of towns are *always* taken from the language of their founders? It certainly is not. All through the western states of America can be found towns with Indian and Spanish names, but the Indians and Spanish had nothing to do with their founding.

The results of constructive reasoning should not be confounded with facts established by direct testimony. In some cases, the conditions may be such that our inference possesses a very high degree of probability, almost certainty, but even then a slight element of doubt remains. For this reason, a synthesis based largely on constructive reasoning can never have the scientific value of one based on the testimony of eye-witnesses. In the next stage in the process of historical reconstruction, the grouping of the facts, this distinction between the two classes of material should always be kept consciously in mind.

VII

SYNTHESIS, OR GROUPING OF THE FACTS

THE preceding step in method leaves us with a heterogeneous mass of data, some of which are certain, many only probable. It is now in order to organize these data into a complex, unique, evolving whole, the parts of which stand in causal relation to each other.

Although for the purpose of exposition it is usual and necessary to treat successively the steps in historical method, as if each step were completed before the next had been begun, in practice this is not true. The grouping of the facts begins at the very outset of the investigation. The reading of a single source gives us our first idea of the subject as a whole and with that conception in mind we read the next source, modifying our first conception to bring it into harmony with the new evidence. And so the process goes on, weaving back and forth, from the fact to the general conception and from the general conception back to the new fact, until all the data have been examined and the general conception is complete. This first, unconscious synthesis is not a critically constructed whole; it will be modified later by the criticism of the documents and by the establishment of the facts, but the large outlines of the subject will not, probably, be very much changed.

It is with this general conception in mind, the by-product of the preceding steps, that we turn to examine carefully the data resulting from criticism, (1) to set bounds to our subject, (2) to divide it into periods, (3) to decide what facts are to form part of the synthesis and what are to be discarded, (4) what causal connection exists between the parts, (5) what change has been effected by the historic action, (6) what parts shall be emphasized and what touched upon but lightly and, finally, (7) how many data shall be used for the sake of color to produce verisimilitude in the reproduction of the past.

The first practical problem to be dealt with is the limitation of the subject. An historical episode has theoretically no beginning and no end, everything being in turn both cause and effect. But while the world's history runs on without break from beginning to end, a careful examination of the whole movement reveals acts and scenes in great variety, offering to the investigator the possibility of limiting his work. For limitation is imperatively necessary, if the investigator is to penetrate below the surface. Every historian cannot write a history of the world based upon first-hand information; he must limit himself to a scene or an act, he must begin somewhere and end somewhere. He must drive a stake in the glacier of time to mark the beginning of his task and one to mark its end.

These dates do not fix the limits, but are themselves fixed by our conception of what constitutes the unity of our subject. If we are dealing with the foundation of the German empire, the question is, where did the movement begin that terminated in the German empire and at what time did that movement culminate, that is, at what time was the empire established. The last date is not difficult to fix, being found in the proclamation of the empire, but just where the movement began is a matter more difficult to deal with. It certainly had begun when the Schleswig-Holstein question became an issue between Prussia and Austria in 1865, but our synthesis would probably have to go farther back and deal with the organization of the Prussian army and probably even farther still to the failure to establish the empire in 1849.

If our subject were the French revolution, we should have some difficulty in fixing both beginning and end. Our treatment could hardly begin with 1789; it must go back at least to 1787 and the assembly of the notables, if it is to be intelligible, even to 1774, to Turgot and his reforms (1774). For an understanding of the formation of public opinion and the rôle of the parlements, our search for origins may take us back to 1748. At the other end, it would be difficult to decide where to stop short of 1795. If we pass 1795, there are weighty reasons for not stopping at 1799.

In dealing with the whole problem, whether we shall embrace more or less in a synthesis, we are inevitably influenced, if we are to write a book or a thesis, by the practical consideration of the number of pages we have at our disposal. This is true even of the paper of an undergraduate. If the space is limited and the treatment of the subject aims to be full, then the scope must be limited to make possible a full and detailed treatment. But this practical limitation in the formulation of the results of our research, the limitation that announces to us, "You must say what you have to say in five thousand words; see that you waste none of them," is after all a secondary matter. The primary question is, if we have material enough for a paper of ten thousand words and must limit ourselves to five thousand, what shall be retained and what discarded? How shall we discriminate between the essential and the unessential? It is the question of values, the fundamental question in historical synthesis and the one concerning which there is least agreement among historians today.

What is the meaning of the term *value* in historical construction? Clearly not the expression of opinion as to whether a certain fact or group of facts is good or bad, useful or useless today, but whether the fact or group has any importance for a given synthesis and, hence, should form an integral part of it.

It is a teleological question, for, in the last analysis, the whole question of historical synthesis is a teleological question. Not, for the most part, a question of what should be the goal of man's unique activity in society, but what has been the goal; what, in specific cases, was the end aimed at and attained by man's unique, social activity.

For instance, man's unique social activities built up the Roman empire, formed united Italy and united Germany and transformed the thirteen English colonies in North America into a nation. The unification of Italy is an accomplished fact, the result of conscious effort aimed at the accomplishment of a definite end. Assuming that it has historical value, that is, is an important fact in European history, the historian attempts to show how it was attained. What facts shall enter into his synthesis? If no limit were set to the length of the exposition, it would include all acts that contributed to the unification of Italy and that should, therefore, appear as parts of the complex whole which we call a synthesis. But if the length of the exposition is limited, then it becomes necessary to distinguish the more important from the less important facts.

The limitations placed upon the exposition will not permit, for example, the inclusion both of the conference between Napoleon and Cavour at Plombières and the unsuccessful revolutionary undertaking of Mazzini in Genoa. Which shall be omitted? The problem is not solved by our interest in Cavour or Mazzini, but by our estimate of the importance of these specific acts for the end in view, namely, the unification of Italy, and without hesitation we treat the interview of Plombières as the more important; without it, what followed would not be intelligible.

Again, the problem of value might be one of emphasis and not of omission. Both facts may and should be included, but one may be more fully developed than the other. Which should receive the fuller development? Evidently the one that played the more important part in bringing about unification.

To say that in order to determine what facts shall enter into a synthesis and which of these facts shall be emphasized the historian must see the subject as a whole, would seem to be equivalent to saying that the synthesis must exist before it is created. For if the synthesis is made up of facts selected by the historian because of their value for the whole, he must know what the whole is before he selects his facts to compose it. But like many another logical dilemma this one is not so serious as it seems.

In practice, the historian begins his research with some general idea of the whole subject obtained from secondary works. As he reads over the sources he has gathered, the original conception of the whole is constantly being enlarged and corrected, and this enlarged and corrected whole reacts upon the work of collecting and interpreting the evidence. Evidence which was considered highly important, in the early stages of the investigation, may lose in importance as the result of further study, while facts considered unimportant at first, may, in a later stage, become highly important. When the evidence is all in, the problem of what the whole is and what facts are important for the whole has been solved in a rough way. The formal outline serves as a court of final revision in which the entire ground is gone over again and earlier judgments confirmed or reversed.

Assuming the value of Italian unification for European history, the problem of synthesis raises no metaphysical difficulty. But suppose its value were doubted, how could it be demonstrated? Simply by considering the importance of the realization of Italian unity for the understanding of that larger whole, of which it forms a part, European history. If one of the ends—and a very important one—of man's unique social activity in Europe is the formation of a united Europe, then it should be clear that the unification of Italy and the unification of Germany are important steps in that teleological process, are important facts, valuable for the larger synthesis. In the same way, we would test the value of European history for the largest possible synthesis, a world history.

If no metaphysical elements have appeared, up to this point, in the treatment of the logic of the synthesis, it is partly due to the fact of the limitation of the field dealt with in the synthesis. This will become clear, if we consider the problem of a synthesis of the world's history as a complex whole and not simply from the point of view of outward unity and social framework. Let us face the problem at once by asking: What shall enter into a history of the world? Shall it deal with all sides of man's unique development, economic, educational, political, scientific, artistic, philosophical and religious or with only one or two of these, the economic and political, for example? If with all, where is the emphasis to be laid? Which of these activities is the more important? Important for what? Here we are in the very inner sanctuary of metaphysics.

It should become clear that the construction of a world synthesis presupposes a philosophy of life. Is society, in all its outward manifestations, an end in itself or only a means to an end? If so, what is that end? Is it, as Eucken has said, "the development of a spiritual content in life"? Is the chief end of man's unique social activity the development of human personality to the highest point? Is there any possible proof of this? But if it is only a working hypothesis, has it any less reality than if it could be demonstrated? Can man, in his unique activities as a social being, escape the formation of a working hypothesis.

If, on the other hand, he approached the historic reality with the assumption that life is purely materialistic, that man, society and all the tangible and intangible products of man's social activities will finally disappear, has he done anything more than

[133]

form a working hypothesis? And when he formulates the one or the other is he doing anything more or anything less than expressing his opinion upon the meaning of history as a whole, upon the philosophy of history? Has he not always done so? Could he and can he escape doing so? What are the so-called political, economic and religious interpretations of history, if not expressions of a philosophy of life?

In forming the synthesis of the world's history, then, the ground for the choice of data to enter into it still remains one of value, but we can no longer agree upon what the whole is. If the end is in view and is, for example, the unification of Italy, we have firm ground to stand upon. But what is the end of the world's history? If we must wait until the end is reached before we write the world's history, unable before we know the end to determine what the important facts are, no mortal will ever write it. The basis for the choice of our facts must be, in the case of universal history, the thing aimed at, rather than the thing accomplished.

What a world's history shall be, will depend upon the philosophy of life of the writer of the history. What significance would the burning of Giordano Bruno at Rome have for the historian with a materialistic philosophy of life? Why should a man sacrifice his life for an idea! What meaning would the statue of Bruno, erected upon the spot where he was burned at the stake, have for the historian who attached no vital significance to the deeds of the spirit? Would the heaping of flowers on the bronze tablet marking the spot where Savonarola was burned, not bring a pitying smile to his face? The conception of values, determined by the working hypothesis of the meaning of history as a whole, will naturally influence the entire synthesis of history. Such a conception of values the people of each generation has had and the people of every generation must have, if it will give unity to its life's work.

As a rule, the historian does not go to world history for his standards of value. He is supposed to have met all practical requirements, if he has grasped as a whole the period he is describing and introduced into his synthesis only such facts as are important for the teleological appreciation of the whole. He does not incorporate into his synthesis everything he encounters on his way, no matter how interesting, but only such facts as constitute the very bone and tissue of the structure he is building. It is sufficiently difficult to conform even to this standard; in fact, most historians fall far short of it.

To know that certain facts should form part of an historical synthesis is one thing; to know how to combine these facts so that they will form a complex whole is quite another. Investigation has placed in our hands a great mass of facts, economic, political and religious. How shall they be arranged within the limits we have set for the study? Shall we narrate them in the chronological order in which they happened, one after the other, doing the work of an annalist? In that case, we should lay ourselves open to the well-known criticism that "facts and facts do not constitute history." The whole must have logical unity, the facts must be presented in their causal connection. Logical unity demands that facts of the same kind should be grouped together; causal connection assumes that the facts will be so arranged as to make clear how one complex situation grows out of the preceding complex situation. To meet these requirements, the facts must be arranged in series and the series must be combined into a complex, causally connected whole.

Let us take as an illustration the period of the French revolution lying between July, 1787, and July, 1790. This forms a natural whole. The first date marks the demand of the parlement of Paris for the calling of the states general which, as the constituent assembly, was to make a constitution and transform France; the last date is that of the great celebration on the Champ de Mars, when delegations from all parts of France gathered around the altar of the country and solemnly swore to maintain the constitution which had been made by the national assembly.

This larger period falls naturally into two of unequal length; the first, extending from July, 1787, to July, 1789, has to do with the history of the states general and its transformation into a national assembly, ending with the revolution of July, 1789; the second, covering a period of one year, was marked

by the abolition of privileges and the reorganization
and unification of France. To synthesize the first
period is a matter of no great difficulty, as we have
to do largely with a single series; in the second
period, however, the increased complexity of the
subject matter increases the number of series and
consequently the difficulty of synthesizing them.

The first step toward the solution of the problem
is to ascertain how many series will be needed and to
construct the various series in turn, tracing the single
thread through the whole period. We should then
have, for example, a political series, falling into the
sub-series of (1) the policy of the king and court, (2)
the policy of Necker and his associates, (3) the attempts of members of the assembly to form a ministry, (4) the work of the assembly in reorganizing
and governing France and (5) the application of
the new constitution; an economic series, with the
sub-series (1) feudal rights, (2) finance, (3) church
and state lands, (4) food supply and (5) the unem-
ployed; an ecclesiastical series dealing with (1)
the abolition of the clergy as an order, (2) the abolition of monasteries and convents, (3) the seizure
and sale of church property, (4) the civil constitution of the clergy and (5) the relations of France to
the papacy. The fifth subdivision would divide again
into (a) the relations of the clergy with the pope,
(b) the relations of the king with the pope and (c)
the official relations of the ministry with the pope.
Each one of these sub-series should be worked out as

a causal development in chronological order, the sub-series combined into a series and the series into the final complex whole.

In selecting from a mass of facts those which are to form parts of an historical series, the historian has to do with the first logical distinction between the synthesis of history and the synthesis of natural science. *The method of doing a thing is determined by what one wants to do.* A logical method is one which adapts means to ends the most successfully and with the least expenditure of effort. The aim of the natural scientist is to organize reality through an understanding of what objects have in common. These resemblances form the basis of generaliza-tions—laws—more or less comprehensive and these in turn make prediction possible. It is noted that when the same conditions are reproduced, the same results follow.

The historian, on the contrary, is interested in what the natural scientist passes by. His object is not to note resemblances, but differences; not to formulate generalizations—laws—but to construct complex, unique wholes. The aims being different, the methods are necessarily different.

Both the historian and the natural scientist—here the sociologist—must use past social facts, both must establish the truth of their facts by the application of critical methods, but the moment the work of syn-thesis begins they part company. In deciding what human activities—whether of individuals or of groups—shall enter into his complex synthesis, the historian is not guided by what these activities have in common with other activities, but by the individual characteristics *distinguishing* them from other activities. Luther's importance for the reformation is not found in what his activities had in common with other Germans of his day, but in acts that were peculiarly his own. The sociologist may be interested, in a legitimate way, in what the French revolution has in common with other revolutions, but the business of the historian is to trace its characteristic differences. These differences can not be formulated as laws, but must be described as parts of a complex, unique, changing whole. As the historian searches through past social facts, he constantly asks himself: "Which of these facts are important for the complex, unique whole I am trying to construct? Which should form a part of it and how important a part?" The facts selected, he endeavors to arrange them in the form of causally connected series.

In the treatment of a sub-series, the facts of the series should be arranged in chronological order for study, in order to determine the number of main groups into which the series should be divided. As, for example, in dealing with the work of the French national assembly in making a constitution, we would have the creation of a first committee and its report, the creation of a second committee and its report, the declaration of rights, the foundations of the constitution, the division of France into departments and districts and the creation of municipalities. Each of these heads in turn would become a main head under which the facts would be grouped and this subdivision would be continued until we reach the single undivided fact.

But even the single series is not free from the perplexities due to parallel activities. For example, before the legislation on departmental organization was completed, the assembly began the consideration of municipal organization and up to the end of December, 1789, both subjects occupied the attention of the assembly. Here the rational course is to make two sub-series, following the debates on each to the end, that is, to the passing of the decrees creating departments and municipalities, then to combine these sub-series, in the order (1) departments, (2) municipalities, and to incorporate them into the larger outline of the political activities. This will necessitate some chronological overlapping, but that is inevitable in any good synthesis.

The grouping of single facts in the smallest subdivision of the series will call for a re-examination of the pages of the notebook in which the facts were established with the citation of the sources. It is wise, when the facts have been given their place in the outline, to transfer to the outline at the same time the references to the sources. They may be inserted on the right-hand side of the outline or entered on a sheet arranged to face the outline, the connection between the outline and the references being marked by figures attached to the facts of the outline and pre-fixed to the notes. When the exposition is reached, the references are all at hand and may be readily appended to the text.

Several historical series, no matter how well worked out, do not constitute a historical synthesis. To finish the work, these series must be combined into an organic whole. This is the most difficult part of the synthesis and is seldom accomplished in an ideal manner. A succession of unrelated chapters printed together in a book do not, for that reason, constitute an organic whole. The history of Europe, for example, is something more than the histories of the countries of Europe and something different from these; if it were not, there would be no reason for attempting to write it. Although a volume made up of unrelated chapters, if each chapter is well or-ganized, represents an advance over the volume in which the facts are simply narrated in their chrono-logical order, it is only a torso.

How can the different series be combined into an organic whole? By bringing them into vital relation with each other and by shifting the narrative from one series to another as the interest shifts. Follow one series as long as it occupies the center of the stage, allowing the other series to drop out of sight. When the interest shifts to another series, drop the first, but before following the new series from the point where it impinges on the old, pick up as many of the back threads of the new series as may be necessary for the understanding of what is to follow.

Suppose, for example, we have narrated the history of the states general of 1789, as far as the uprising of July of that year. The interest, up to that time, had been centered at Versailles. It now passes to Paris and from Paris to France. Shall we continue to follow the events in Versailles and Paris, or turn to the provinces and trace the course of the municipal revolution, "the great fear," the arming of the peasants and the attack on the châteaux? The assembly had begun to make the constitution and was discussing the declaration of rights. Important as this was, what was going on in the provinces was bigger and more important. Moreover, the movement in the provinces was such a natural result of the Paris uprising that it would be a violation of historical continuity as well as an error in the judgment of values not to follow this movement to the frontiers instead of remaining quietly in Versailles, listening to the debates of the assembly.

Artistic reasons might also be adduced for following this order. How effective the presentation is which follows the great sweep of the revolution over the provinces, describes the destruction of the feudal records by the peasants, the accompanying disorders, the return wave to Versailles, the reports of violence flowing in upon the assembly from all sides, the creation of a committee to examine them, its reports on August 3, the revised report on the night of

August 4, and the opening of the dramatic scene that ended with the sweeping away of the remnants of feudal rights in France! How much more effective such a synthesis is than one which follows the acts of the assembly to the last of July, without recounting the revolution in the provinces, and only when the reports of violence begin to come in turns back to pick up the threads, to recount the great July revolution, the arming of the peasants and the practical destruction of feudalism.

Following the first order, after dealing with the debates on feudal rights and the voting of the final decree, we would turn to the work on the constitution, recall the reports of the two committees created in July, the debates on the advisability of formulating a declaration of rights, and then go on to consider the debates on the declaration itself, leaving the events in the provinces behind the scene. Versailles once more holds the center of the stage. The question under discussion,—after the declaration had been disposed of,—"Shall the king have the veto power?" aroused a feverish interest in the people of France. It involved the problem of the limitation of arbitrary power, one of the two great problems of the revolution.

At the close of the debates on the foundations of the constitution, Paris thrust itself into the foreground by the insurrection of October 5, 1789, and an opportunity is given to consider the questions of food supply; the intrigues of the court; the reactionary movement in the assembly; the distrust of the people of Paris and their desire to have the king in Paris, a desire entertained also by the French Guards, former guards of the king at Versailles, now the paid nucleus of the Paris militia; the calling of the regiment of Flanders, and the banquet given by the king's bodyguard on October 1. All of these events are causes of the insurrection, must be dealt with to bring the insurrection into causal connection with the larger revolutionary movement and form important sub-series naturally considered at the point where they impinge on the political series under consideration.

To decide how far back each of these sub-series should be followed, how fully it should be treated and how the sub-series can be combined into a complex causally related whole is a task of no little difficulty. The practical consideration of space limitations—number of pages and words in the finished study—must always be kept in mind and good judgment must be exercised in eliminating unimportant matter to make room for more important. The subject must be so thoroughly mastered as a whole and in detail that there will be no uncertainty about chronological order and as little as possible about causal connection.

The assembly was engaged in making a constitution. The connecting link between this series and the events of October 5 and 6 is found in the belief of the people of Paris that the national assembly was becoming reactionary. It was also reported in Paris that the king was planning a flight to Metz. This situation gave birth to the idea that the king and assembly should be brought to Paris. The French Guards encouraged this idea that they might resume their posts as royal guards held before the July insurrection. An attempt on the part of the guards to go to Versailles to bring the king to Paris was thwarted by Lafayette, but led to the strengthening of the garrison of Versailles by the calling of the regiment of Flanders.

The banquet of October 1, given in the theatre of the château to the officers of the new regiment by the bodyguards of the king, was evidently intended to create a sentiment of attachment to the royal family. Reports that the national assembly had been omitted from the toasts, that the tricolored cockade had been trampled under foot and pronounced anti-revolutionary sentiment shown in other ways aroused the indignation of the people of Paris and rendered a popular outbreak highly probable.

The immediate cause of the insurrection is found in the lack of bread, and an account of the rôle played in the history of Paris during the summer of 1789 by the defective food supply naturally ends with a description of the first fact in the uprising, the arrest of the baker of Saint-Eustache, in the early morning of October 5, charged with selling bread under weight. From this beginning, the events of October 5 and 6 follow in a natural causal order.

The combination of single facts into series and series into complex wholes implies causal connection. In history, as in natural science, there is no effect without a cause, but causality in natural science expresses itself as causal law—the effect being equal to the cause—while in history it takes the form of causal connection, one complex group being the effect of that which precedes it. The statement that the cause is always equal to the effect is true of a synthesis in natural science, but not of an historical synthesis. In history, a small cause—the resentment of Madame de Pompadour—may produce a great effect, or a great cause may be utterly without effect. The cause could be equal to the effect only in a system of logic from which the individual, the unique, had been eliminated. The causal law is part of a system which concerns itself with resemblances, notes repetitions and formulates generalizations or laws.

To both systems—natural science and historical science—causality applies. There is nothing without cause either in natural science or in historical science, but in natural science causality finds expression in the law that the cause is always equal to the effect, while in historical science it takes the shape of causal connection.

To the historian, it is interesting to know that a lighted match thrown into a barrel of shavings may destroy a great city; he has convincing proof that the thing has been done. To the objection of the natural scientist that this is an insufficient explanation of what has taken place, he replies that it is quite sufficient in a system which takes account only of the individual, which is concerned with noting how each occurrence differs from every other, with grasping the whole in its complexity. He acknowledges that it is interesting and important to know that in this fire can be found something common to all fires, a law of combustion, but when the knowledge sought relates to the unique it is not to be satisfied by information concerning the general. The natural scientist may discover his causal law at work by eliminating from the problem all that is individual, all that interests the historian, retaining only what is common to all conflagrations and this causal law will be quite as true, in its way, as the historian's causal connection: the one supplements the other.

It is not incumbent upon the historian, then, to seek for laws; it is incumbent upon him to show causal connection, to make clear that one group of facts is in causal connection with another group, to bind all the groups together causally from the beginning to the end of the synthesis. In such a synthesis there should be nothing isolated, no flotsam and jetsam of curious facts, but all should be held together in a necessary connection in which each fact has its place. To the question, "Is such a synthesis possible?" one would make answer as Ranke did to the query whether a universal history such as he had conceived could be written: "It must, perforce," he replied, "be attempted."

Improvement in historical synthesis means an approach to this goal. With each generation, the facts are established with more certainty, the series are worked out in greater fulness and some advance is made in the effort to combine these series into a complete causally connected whole. If we would not attempt too much, but would be content with a small piece of work well done, the greater synthesis would advance more rapidly.

It is only through causal connection that an event becomes intelligible. Detach the French revolution in France from its relations with Europe—from the foreign wars—and the uprisings of June 20 and August 10, 1792, the September massacres and the reign of terror become unintelligible; they seem the work of men demented. The explanation of a narrative made up of disconnected episodes, of unexplained events, is found in a lack of knowledge; the remedy is further research.

For a long time it was said in explanation of the conquest of the Greek world by Philip of Macedon that the Greeks were no longer the men of Marathon and Salamis; more thorough investigation has found the cause in the unequal struggle of a disunited group of small states against a territorial monarchy with large resources in men and money, ruled by a great soldier and statesman.

The federation of the Champ de Mars of July 14, 1790, is usually presented as a spectacular event, innocent of all connection with what had preceded it, bursting upon our unprepared vision like a rocket exploding in a dark night. What a different impression the event makes when we see it as the culmination of a movement that was the outcome of the July uprising of 1789, small in its beginnings, growing steadily more general, month by month, embracing greater areas and larger bodies of men, until it sweeps in like a great wave upon Paris. Thus conceived, it becomes one of the most significant and thrilling events not only of the French revolution, but of the entire history of France, it marks the birth of the spiritual unity of the French people, the outcome of eighteen centuries of French history.

There are many events like this, forming the termination of a long causal series running through centuries. To the scientific mind, the seizure of Rome by the Italians in the fall of 1870 is fully intelligible only when the causal connection has been traced back to Pippin and to the creation of the temporal power of the popes. If it is said that it is easier to see such causal connection when it has been pointed out than it is to discover it for one's self, the answer would be that if sufficient evidence exists to enable the investigator to establish the facts and combine them into series, if he will gaze long and attentively at his series, if he will but press them for their larger significance and causal connection, he will seldom fail to get his reward.

There are things, however, that cannot be taught, that can find no place in formal method. The great historian adds to his knowledge of method, an insight, a genius for seeing wholes in scattered fragments, of detecting causal connections that makes a great and vital synthesis possible. He is a great artist as well as a great scientist. Much instruction may be found, by him for whom the talent of hard work must take the place of genius, in the synthesis of historians like Ranke, who has given us so many classical examples of the grouping of masses of facts into organic wholes. The young student of history could hardly do better than go to school to him, to learn from his great narratives the technique of a great master.

A well-organized synthesis must do something more than present a series of events in causal connection; it must also display unique change. For unique change is one of the essential characteristics of history. History is dynamic; it deals with mankind in action and its purpose is to trace the unique changes which are the result of these activities. In real life, a group of individuals, living under certain unique conditions, moved by certain motives, act in an individual way and modify the social conditions existing when the action began. Any synthesis that does not make clear these three things, (1) the original condition, (2) the action and (3) the novelty in the resulting conditions fails to meet the legitimate demands of historical method. So long as these results are made clear it is a matter of indifference what the peculiar form of the synthesis is.

The simplest and traditional form of synthesis, consisting of a full description of the institutions of a period and the public discontent to which they gave birth, followed by an account of the series of actions that reorganized society and a description of the new society, may not be the most effective form of presentation. A synthesis which associates the change (the action) with an account of the institution changed and the form into which it was changed has much more organic unity. Many of the older histories of the French revolution which began with a description of the abuses of the old society and of the birth of a critical public opinion failed to develop any organic connection between this first part of the synthesis and the revolutionary activity which followed; they omitted entirely any account of the transformed society which resulted from the revolutionary activity. In dealing with the church and the French revolution, for example, a full description of the old ecclesiastical organization and of all the accompanying abuses is not essential to a general synthesis of the revolution, but only those parts need to be described which were affected by the revolution.

A closer unity between the parts of the synthesis is secured if description and action are associated, description being introduced at the point where action is about to transform a condition. For example, an account of the French revolution might well reach the uprising of July, 1789, without making mention of feudal rights; the attack of the peasants on the

[151]

châteaux and the action of the assembly offer opportunity for as much explanation, and in immediate connection with the act, as may be found necessary to understand the act and the characteristic features of the new condition created by the act.

But whatever the form of synthesis used, the threefold aim should not be forgotten. No useless baggage should be taken aboard, no data should be included in the synthesis which do not show what the original conditions were, by what acts they were changed and what the changes were. Furthermore, there should be no missing links. That is, there should be no description of conditions unaffected by transforming acts, no acts without antecedents in conditions, and no changed conditions not accounted for by previous acts and conditions.

A synthesis may be successful in showing fulness of series, causal connection and unique change and yet be badly proportioned, as a result of a failure to distinguish between important and unimportant factors and events. Not that historical facts are big *per se;* they are important because of what they accomplish and they are emphasized not by rhetorical flourish in the form of personal judgment, but by a detailed presentation which makes clear how they accomplished what they did accomplish. The detail with which an event or a topic is treated, the larger or smaller space devoted to it in the outline, is indicative, or should be indicative, of the importance attached to it by the historian. To give undue prominence to details, because they are curious or dramatic, is to throw the picture out of perspective and is a mark of poor workmanship.

Finally, some space in the outline should be devoted to material introduced for the purpose of securing local color, of giving an air of verisimilitude to the reproduction of the past. How far this material should be employed cannot be determined by rule; it is a matter of good judgment and artistic taste. It must not be allowed to crowd out more important details showing causal connection, nor can it be permitted to usurp the space which should be used to give emphasis to some important topic. The choice of the details to produce color is also a matter of taste. What is the effect one wishes to produce? What details may be used to produce that effect? How many of these details do we need to employ?

In speaking of the opening of the states general of 1789 we might say: "The procession of the estates, which marked the opening of the states general, took place at Versailles on May 4, in the presence of an enthusiastic throng of people." Here there is little for the imagination to work upon; characteristic details are necessary. They would consist of references (1) to the beauty of the day, (2) to the crowds filling the windows along the route of the procession—high price of seats—and even gathering on the housetops and peering from the chimney-pots; (3) to the houses hung with tapestries and the double lines of troops along the route of the procession; (4) to the starting point and goal of the procession, the two churches of Nôtre-Dame and Saint-Louis; (5) to the order of the procession, headed by chanting monks, followed by the third estate (description of dress), the nobility (description of dress), the clergy (description of dress), and the court, all carrying tapers; (6) to bands of music; (7) to the gaiety of the crowd and the reception of the king and queen and of the different orders and individuals. Many of these details, such as the treatment of the king and queen, of the Duc d'Orleans, of the third estate by the crowd, the difference in dress, the attempts to impress upon the deputies of the third estate the fact that they occupied an inferior position in society, serve the double purpose of giving color and aiding in the development of causally connected series. Color may also be secured by the description of the physical setting of the event or by the use of contemporary illustrations. The *Révolutions de Paris,* for example, has an excellent series of contemporary woodcuts, dealing with the striking events of the revolution.

In its final form, the synthesis will appear as a detailed, well-organized outline, showing the results of the investigation as a unique, complex whole and indicating, after each detail in the outline, where the information was found that made possible the establishment of that particular fact. This outline forms the skeleton, the bone and muscle, to be clothed with flesh and blood by the exposition or narrative.

VIII

EXPOSITION

It is sometimes said that when the synthesis is completed the exposition will offer little difficulty. I recall making some such statement myself years ago in striving to impress upon my pupils the importance of a thoroughly prepared outline. I should have told them that if they had mastered their outline, had all the evidence in mind, could see the subject as a whole and the relative importance of the parts, if they had sufficient command of the English language to express exactly what they had in mind, sufficient knowledge of the technique of rhetoric to present the subject as a unit, the writing of the narrative would be comparatively easy! A knowledge of historical method does not imply the possession of a large and varied vocabulary, or skill in the nice use of words, and without these the result of historical research cannot be adequately expressed. This condition is not peculiar to historical narration, but is common to all prose exposition.

The necessity of adequate literary expression for the results of historical research in no wise justifies the assumption that history is literature or that the historical narrative is a failure if it is not a work of art. The assumption is false and betrays a false conception of what should be required of an historical narrative. History certainly is not fiction and no amount of style can redeem a work that is not true, that is, as true as it is possible to make it. *The first question to be asked of every historical work is not Is it interesting and well written? but Is it true?* That the results of historical research should, if possible, have adequate literary expression goes without saying. For the historian, as for the literary artist, "structure is all-important . . . that architectural conception of work, which forsees the end in the beginning and never loses sight of it and in every part is conscious of all the rest, till the last sentence does but, with undiminished vigor, unfold and justify the first." Both must insist on "unity" and "vital wholeness," but that agreement does not make literature of history.

An historical work is not a unique, detached thing, complete in itself, like a sonnet, a picture or a statue. It is part of a larger body of historical truth; it is attached to what has gone before and to what follows it. The aim of the historian is not to arouse the emotions, but to convince the intellect of the truth of his exposition of some period of man's unique social evolution. If the final exposition of his work is dramatic or has artistic unity, it is purely an accident. The historian does not search for dramatic episodes; his subject may not lend itself to dramatic treatment and if it should, in part, it is highly improbable that the source material would make possible the perfect execution of the conception. The work would remain a torso.

The literary artist may draw upon his imagination; the historian can draw only on his sources, and when the sources fail, his work is at an end. His use of the imagination is purely scientific; it helps him to revive what has existed, to visualize the facts established by the sources and to conceive the whole composed of the facts. An uncontrolled, subconscious imagination may make a good artist, but it makes a very poor historian. The work of the historian is not creative in the artistic sense.

The false assumption that history is a branch of literature, that an historical narrative must be a work of art, has seriously hampered the progress of scientific historical work. It leaves the field open to a horde of amateurs whose only equipment is facility in writing and encourages the pernicious inference that every history should be written for the general public. No amount of fine writing can give any value to an historical work that is not true. It is extraordinary that it should be necessary to insist upon this point; it should be self-evident. Who would think of saying of a work on chemistry or botany or physics, "I don't know how sound it is, but it is brilliantly written and interesting," and believe they were saying anything of fundamental importance concerning the scientific value of the work? What layman would even think of passing a judgment upon a scientific work—a volume on natural science—or would think himself justified in complaining because it was not as interesting as a novel or as easily understood?

What is the explanation of this difference in the attitude of the public toward natural and historical science? *It is due to the absolute ignorance of the public of what historical science is or of the existence even of historical science.* So long as it is assumed that anybody can write history and that anybody can teach history and in neither case any technical training is looked upon as indispensable, just so long will the shelves of our libraries be crowded with so-called histories, unsound from cover to cover, showing nothing so clearly as the incompetence of the writer, and so long will the public go on estimating the value of an historical work by its style and attractiveness.

Drive the "history fakir" from the field of historical writing and the untrained history teacher from the schoolroom and the educated public of the next generation will take a different attitude toward historical work and have a better appreciation of the difficulties of historical research. Then it will be possible for the public to understand that it is no more reasonable to expect that all historical work should be written for the general reader than that all works on natural science should be accessible to the same class of readers.

Should there be, then, no popular histories, histories for general readers? Undoubtedly there should be such books, free from footnotes, bibliographies and all scientific apparatus, but containing the truth of the latest investigations upon the topic treated. There is no more justification for an untrue popular history than for an untrue scientific history. No man is forced to become an interpreter to the public of what scientific historians have written; no man is justified in undertaking to play the rôle unless he is something more than a ready writer; he must know his subject and know it as the scholar knows it. The ideal condition would be to have the scientific and popular histories written by the same man; first the careful investigation of the subject and a scientific exposition of the results for the benefit of scholars and then a popular presentation of the same matter for the general public.

One thing, above all others, should be clear; the scholar should never attempt to reach both audiences in the same book; his scientific work is bound to suffer. A distinguished German historian of the last generation published a volume embodying the results of long years of research; the footnotes were relegated to the back of the book. "I want readers," was the excuse that he gave. Others have gone farther and entirely eliminated all footnotes, all proof of the truth of the statements made in the text.

What could be more unscholarly, more lacking in appreciation of the conditions of progress in historical knowledge? How can an exposition of that character extend the bounds of *demonstrated* historical truth? The reader asks: "What evidence did the historian have before him? how exhaustive was his research? how critically did he use his material?" How is it possible to answer these questions, if the narrative is not accompanied, step by step, by the evidence? What help can such an exposition be to the later investigator of the same period? How can he tell what was well and finally done and what remains to be done? Only by going over the entire field again. To present the results of long years of scientific research in unscientific form is but to waste the time of the investigator and the time of those who come after him. And what is gained by it? Nothing. The reader who would be frightened from a page because he is confronted by footnotes is too much of an intellectual weakling to deserve serious consideration. The duty of the scientist is first of all to his science. *The results of scientific research must be formulated scientifically and that can be done only by the investigator*. The popular exposition may be prepared by another, if the investigator is unable to undertake it.

We are not concerned, then, as scholars, with a popular history for general readers, but with the exposition of the results of scholarly historical research. It should be the work of a scholar done for scholars. Such an exposition consists of (1) a prose narrative, (2) footnotes and (3) appendixes consisting of bibliographies, documents and critical discussions. Let us consider the nature of each in turn.

What should be the characteristics of the narrative? First of all it should possess "vital wholeness."

How can that be secured? One would think it only necessary to piece together the items of the outline, thus creating the whole of which they are the parts. Unfortunately this is not true. To present the incidents of the outline, one after the other, without connecting or explanatory matter will either lead to the swamping of the reader in a mass of details or will force him to work out the connections for himself. The narrative consists of the outline plus the connecting tissue, the explanation which enables the reader to grasp the organization, the unity underlying the text. The reader has not examined the sources, he has not accompanied the historian in the work of construction; he does not have the detailed outline before him, and yet the historian wishes to convey to his mind the general view of the subject that has taken shape in his own mind as the result of his investigations.

To make clear the unity he has discovered in the mass of details, the historian must begin with the whole. He must sketch its limits, its general outline and characteristics, and then, descending to the parts of the whole, he must reveal the individuality of each while describing the facts which constitute it. As he advances step by step, he must help the reader to hold in mind what has been presented and to note the direction in which he is moving. Two indispensable conditions of success in conveying the idea of unity in the work are for the historian to see it himself and to be able to estimate the value of his exposition as a complete and correct expression of the whole he has in mind.

The conception of the subject as a whole calls for the use of the constructive imagination. One must not only keep the whole subject in mind, while the synthesis is taking shape, but long hours of study must be given to the completed outline before the work of exposition begins and the outline must be constantly before the student's eyes while the exposition is in progress. The young student must rid himself of the idea that the outline is something extraneous and not at all indispensable; that it is simply an additional burden inflicted on him by the instructor. *It is the only means of effectively organizing the results of historical study*—or of any other study, for that matter—and without this skeleton to work upon, the imagination may labor in vain.

How much unity the imagination may see in the facts depends upon the imagination. That the imagination may be trained is doubtless true, but no amount of industry or critical skill in establishing the facts can take the place of the scientific imagination in fusing these facts into a whole. This part of the historian's work must depend largely upon genius and genius cannot be taught.

Polybius, profoundly impressed by the dominating position of Rome in the Mediterranean basin, as he saw it with his own eyes, asked himself how it had been attained. The answer to that question, given by his constructive imagination, was the most important work of historical exposition produced by antiquity. Bryce, dwelling upon facts long known and often narrated, saw a vision of the *Holy Roman Empire* which gave unity to a thousand years of European history.

Gibbon had a vision that supplemented the vision of Polybius and described *The Decline and Fall of the Roman Empire,* while Thierry, in his *Tableau de l'empire romain,* described as a whole the two phases of Rome's work which had been treated separately by Polybius and Gibbon.

These are a few, well-known examples of the work of the constructive historical imagination. Everywhere opportunities are offered for synthesis quite as valuable as these, and contributions, on a large or a small scale, to an understanding of the unity of history, in part or as a whole, are made each year. It is this side of exposition, no doubt, that has led to the classification of history as literature and it is the fascination attaching to the exposition of large and significant wholes which has attracted the writer without historical training into the historical field. It must never be forgotten, however, that these brilliant syntheses are valuable only in so far as they take deep root in the critical results of historical investigation and stand the test, in every part, of severe historical criticism.

The ability to visualize the subject as a whole is not the sole condition of a successful exposition; one must be able to criticise his own narrative, to note whether it really reflects the vision of unity, thus making it possible for the reader to see the subject as the investigator has seen it. The most practical way to get a detached point of view is to lay the first draft aside and return to it after it has "become cold." Some approach can be made then to looking at it from the point of view of the uninformed reader and many gaps and obscurities will appear that escaped notice in the heat of the original construction. More *aperçus* to enable the reader to grasp the unity of a group of facts, more connecting observations to enable him to seize the relation between groups, more details to make clear and to demonstrate the truth of an *aperçu*, may be found necessary as the re-result of the rereading of the narrative.

Space will not allow the presentation of specific illustrations of the manner in which the exposition may present the subject as a unit. By studying the narratives of historians who have been markedly successful in this part of the work of reconstruction, one may learn what their technique was. Their methods should not, however, be copied; and after one has made a conscious study of them, he still must learn by writing himself. The difficulty of teaching this part of exposition is due to the fact that every exposition is unique and success or failure will depend upon individual genius.

The problem of unity is not the only one which presses upon the historian who is attempting to give form to the results of his investigation. From the beginning to the end of his narrative he must never lose sight of the fact that he is not speaking with author- ity, but simply stating what he believes to be true from the study of the evidence. It is his business to make clear to the reader just what the condition of the evidence is; whether the statement made in the text is a fact, a probability or the affirmation of a single witness. He is bound to call attention to gaps in the evidence, to an ignorance that cannot be dissi- pated, to problems that need to be solved and possi- ble ways of solving them. These demands made upon the exposition call for slow and wary walking.

It is so easy to make sweeping statements, nearly true, but not quite true; so difficult to hew to the line, neither overstating nor understating, telling neither more nor less than one is justified in telling from the evidence in hand. This critical restraint fre- quently brings the narrative to a halt with the dis- covery of a fresh bit of evidence or with the reali- zation that more evidence ought to be and probably can be found; it even leads to the recasting of por- tions of the narrative when the development of later portions places the earlier portions in a new light. The willingness to submit to this sort of discipline, to meet all these requirements of ideal achievement, are the supreme test of the presence of the scientific spirit in the investigator. In many cases it may be almost an affair of conscience, as nobody may dis- cover some slight defect, if the investigator allows it to pass uncorrected.

The narrative should reflect the character of the evidence. When the matter presented is a fact, supported by the agreement of independent witnesses, it is stated as a fact. For example, in speaking of the calling of the states general of 1789, if we wrote, "The opposition of the parlements forced Louis XVI to summon the states general," the inference would be that the statement rests upon the agreement of the affirmations of independent witnesses. If, on the other hand, we wrote, "It seems probable that the opposition of the parlements forced Louis XVI to call the states general," the critical reader understands that he is not getting a fact, that the affirmations conflict, but that the weight of the testimony seems to favor the statement made. There might be a third case in which one would write, "Sallier states that the opposition of the parlements forced Louis XVI to call the states general," and the reader would understand that Sallier was the only source. Finally, we might say, "There was a rumor," or "it was generally believed, that the opposition of the parlements forced Louis XVI to call the states general," and it would be understood from the form of the statement that the evidence is of very slight value.

It ought to be clear that such a demand for scientific accuracy in a narrative can be met only by one who has made an exhaustive search for sources, has criticised them carefully and has in mind the entire result of that work. Each statement demands the recall of all the evidence and its character. At this point, an historical exposition has nothing in common with a piece of pure literature. The desire to get the proof before the reader will frequently lead to the introduction of documents and source extracts into the text, interrupting the flow of the exposition. This sort of practice shocks the *littérateur,* who prefers to substitute his own paraphrase for the words of the source; to the serious searcher for truth, the evidence incorporated in its original form in the text is as welcome as water to a thirsty land.

Whenever space permits, source material should be incorporated in the text. A paraphrase of a source never has the color of the source itself and there is, furthermore, the possibility of error in condensing. A standard work on European diplomacy states that the French legislative assembly of 1792 voted to declare war on "Austria and the empire"; the text of the declaration states that it was declared upon "the King of Bohemia and Hungary." A quotation of the text of the source would have taken no more space than the false statement.

A narrative cannot, of course, consist of nothing but a collection of source extracts; good judgment is needed to decide what extracts are important enough to use and how much of each shall be used. The practice of weaving sources into the text does not owe its origin to the fact that such a method of construction is easier, calls for less skill in execution than the method of free-flowing narrative which preceded it;

the introduction of evidence in the text is one of the signs of the divorce of history from pure literature and a result of the demand for proof on the part of the reader. The opposition to the method is no better grounded than the opposition to footnotes. Once concede the necessity of demonstrating the truth of the facts composing an historical narrative and one is debarred from objecting to the use of source extracts in the text and of notes at the bottom of the page.

The footnotes should form an integral part of the exposition and offer a sufficient means of controlling the truth of the narrative. One writes more cautiously when one is obliged to cite proof for every statement in the text. The following paragraph, hardly a word of which is true, would never have been written had the writer been obliged to cite his evidence:

"During the applause that followed Necker's address [on May 5, 1789] . . . the king hastily withdrew from the hall, having been warned that Mirabeau was to make himself 'the mouthpiece of the nation's wishes.' The nobility and the clergy immediately followed the king and the deputies of the third estate were left alone in that vast hall. Without leadership or organization, the deputies lingered around for awhile and then gradually melted away."

All of this misstatement and confusion is due to careless and superficial study. The general public alone suffers from such an exposition; it is not in a position to test the truth of the narrative. The student of the French revolution who is even fairly well acquainted with the sources, recognizes at once what he has before him in the paragraph quoted. The general character of the whole volume is one of inaccuracy, and even if the student is not familiar with the evidence touching the Mirabeau incident, but knows what the biographers have written about it, he would not be inclined to believe that this writer, who cites no evidence, had found any unknown to the earlier and more scholarly biographers.

But suppose the passage for which no evidence was cited came from a monographic study by a distinguished historian, published in one of the leading historical reviews; suppose that for other statements in the monograph sources are cited in abundance in footnotes and even hitherto unpublished manuscript material is added in an appendix. Under those circumstances would one not be likely to infer that everything for which evidence was not cited was so well known that citation of evidence seemed superfluous? The inference would not be justified.

In an article on "The Second Ministry of Necker" in the *Revue historique* of May-June, 1891, referring to the royal session of June 23, M. Flammermont wrote: "Tuesday the 23 at eleven o'clock, the king went with great pomp from the château to the hall of the estates . . . Not a single cry was raised to acclaim him." Two sentences and two inaccurate statements: The session was over at eleven o'clock, beginning at half past ten. Camille Desmoulins, who stood outside the hall, wrote to his father the next day: "The king came. As M. Necker did not precede him, we were in consternation. A handful of paid children ran beside the carriage crying, 'Long live the king.' Some valets, some spies joined in the chorus; all respectable people and the crowd remained silent."

How could a scholar as critical as M. Flammermont blunder in this way? On this occasion, M. Flammermont doubtless got his information second-hand and was betrayed by the secondary writer. His failure to examine the sources carefully for the royal session was doubtless due to the fact that he was dealing with Necker, and Necker did not appear at the session. Possibly he used Michelet, who wrote that "even on leaving the château, the king encountered a mournfully silent crowd," and cites Dumont, *Souvenirs sur Mirabeau,* as his source. Dumont, who was an eyewitness, declared that the king received "no applause from the people, not a *vive le roi,*" on leaving the château. This may have been true, but Dumont wrote ten years after the event and had had a good chance to forget. Moreover, what he says about the occurrences at the château does not apply to the whole route from the château to the hall.

The hour of opening an assembly, the cries that did or did not greet a king, are but minor details, and yet if they are of sufficient importance to form part of a narrative, we should know what the evidence is that justifies us in using them as facts. The insistence upon proof for everything will eliminate carelessness even in details. And if the rule of *proof for all statements* is not to apply, where shall the line be drawn? When is a detail so unimportant that the writer may assert it without having proved it? Is it safe under any circumstances to allow the authority of the writer to usurp the place of the authority of the evidence? *There is no authority but the evidence, and the only proof of the scientific good faith of the historian is the citation of the evidence.*

There are three things that may be accomplished by footnotes: (1) The citation of volume and page, etc., indicating where the evidence is found; (2) the quotation of an extract from the source in the exact language of the source; and (3) the discussion of the evidence upon which some statement in the narrative is based. The third kind of a note is the least common and the most difficult to write.

To write the first kind of a note, indicating where the source is to be found, should not be a difficult matter, but an examination of historical narratives would seem to indicate that it is more difficult than it appears. What is the object of such a note? Obviously to enable the reader to find the evidence upon which a statement rests, thus making it possible for him to decide whether the historian was justified in making the statement. The most common reference is to volume and page. Here trouble arises for the reader, if the writer fails to mention the volume, or, if there are several editions of the work, fails to mention the edition used. This latter blunder may make it difficult, sometimes impossible, to find the reference. At times, the volume referred to is rare and it is desirable to refer to the library in which it is found and the library number.

The material used may be manuscript and in such a case the archives or private collection in which it is found should be indicated and the number of the folio, *dossier,* or *carton* should be given, together with the numbering of the particular document. *The reference should be exact enough so that a student on entering the archives could make out his slip and receive the material at once.* For a writer to quote the text of an important document and in his footnote to refer, for example, to the *Archives nationales* is irritating beyond words. How, with no more definite reference than this, can this manuscript be found among the hundreds of thousands of manuscripts making up this great collection? And yet it would have been easy to give the exact reference, for the writer was obliged to use it in order to gain access to the document.

If the monograph is accompained by a critical bibliography, as it should be, giving the full title of the work and indicating where it is found, it is not necessary to repeat the whole of the title in each footnote. In a study on the French revolution, for example, if but one of the works of Necker is used and the title of this is given in full in the bibliography, in the footnotes it may be referred to simply, as *Necker,* — (volume), — (page). No genius is required to write correct notes of this kind; only careful, patient work is necessary. The notes should be *correct* and *definite,* if they are to be of any use; and if they are not intended for use, it would be better to omit them.

The second kind of note, that containing a quotation, also contains the reference to the source. The purpose of this note is to put the exact text of the source before the reader to enable him to judge of the correctness of the inferences drawn from it by the writer. In a scientific work, it should not be a translation, but the source in the original language in which it was recorded, Latin, Greek, French, German, Italian, Spanish, or whatever it may have been. To offer a translation instead of the original text is to leave an element of uncertainty concerning the truth, as the translation may not be exact. Here, again, a correct reproduction of the text is the essential thing and can be accomplished only by one who has a working knowledge of the language.

As a rule, quotations should be made in a note only when the work cited is a rare one or in manuscript form and hence inaccessible to any considerable body of readers, or when it is necessary for the reader to have the text under his eye in order to understand the narrative. The problem of when to introduce the text into the narrative in the form of a translation, if the original is in a foreign language, and when to give it untranslated in a note is a matter which cannot be settled by rule. If the demonstration turns on the exact language of the source, that should be reproduced in a note in the original language, especially if there is any doubt as to what the language means. In the majority of cases it probably would be better to incorporate the quotation in the text.

The last form of footnote, and the most difficult to write, is the critical note. When a statement made in the text is not certain but probable, it is essential that the reader should know not only what the evidence is upon which the statement rests, but also what considerations have led the historian to accept one probability rather than another.

For example, in dealing with the fall of Robespierre, some historians are convinced that he attempted to commit suicide on the morning of the 10th of Thermidor, others believe that he was shot by Méda, while others are unable to reach any conclusion as to the cause of his wound. That he was shot, is certain; who shot him, up to the present time, remains an unsolved problem. In a scientific history of the revolution, a statement that "Robespierre attempted to commit suicide by shooting himself with a pistol, the muzzle of which he placed in his mouth," or that "Robespierre was wounded by the gendarme Méda," or that "it is uncertain whether Robespierre wounded himself or was shot by Méda," should be accompanied by a full critical note of explanation. The note should enumerate the evidence, state the value of it, interpret the affirmations of the witnesses, compare them to determine what the fact is and supplement or control the testimony of the direct witnesses by constructive reasoning. The difficulty of this problem is due to the fact that of the witnesses who knew something about the shooting—Robespierre and Méda—only Méda testified, and when he testified Robespierre was not alive to contradict him.

In his short history of the French revolution Belloc wrote: "As he [Robespierre] sat there with the paper before him and his signature still unfinished, the armed force of the Parliament burst into the room, a lad of the name of Méda aimed a pistol from the door at Robespierre and shot him in the jaw. [The evidence in favor of this version is conclusive.]" In this work, Belloc gives no evidence, but in his life of Robespierre he devotes a note of three pages to a discussion of the evidence. After setting forth some of the statements of contemporaries on either side, he concludes that they contradict each other and that the solution of the problem must be found in the interpretation of the report of the surgeons who examined Robespierre's wound. The wound as they describe it, in the left cheek, could not have been made by a man holding a pistol in his right hand, according to Belloc. Hence Méda must have shot Robespierre.

In writing a history of this episode one might say:

"In the early morning of the 10th of Thermidor, when the troops of the convention entered the city hall, and when his companions were either taking their lives or endeavoring to escape, it seems highly probable that Robespierre attempted to commit suicide by shooting himself with a pistol the muzzle of which was placed in his mouth. He did not kill himself; the bullet shattered his left jaw and passed out through the left cheek, narrowly missing the concierge who was passing. The invaders found Robespierre stretched on the floor bleeding from his wound. One of the first to enter was a gendarme, Méda by name, who claimed later that he found Robespierre seated at a table, that he had words with him and that he finally shot him at close range. This statement, in conflict with all the other evidence, must be dismissed as false."

The proof of these statements might then be given in the following note: There is nothing to confirm the testimony of Méda that he shot Robespierre. According to his account (*Collection des mémoires relatifs à la révolution française. Camille Desmoulins, Vilate et Méda.* Paris, 1825, page 384), as he entered a room in the city hall, he saw some fifty men very much agitated. "In the midst of them, I recognized the elder Robespierre. He was seated in a chair, his left elbow on his knees, his head supported on his left hand. I sprang at him and presenting the point of my saber at his breast said, 'Surrender, traitor!' He raised his head and said to me, 'It is you

who are the traitor and I am going to have you shot.'
At these words, I seized one of my pistols with my
left hand and making a turn to the right, I fired at
him. I intended to shoot him in the breast, but the
ball struck him on the chin and broke his lower jaw;
he fell from his chair.' An examination of the evidence that follows will make clear the ridiculous in-
consistencies of this account.

I have met with one contemporary record which
states that "Robespierre shot himself in the mouth
with a pistol and at the same time was shot by a
gendarme." This statement was made in the convention on the 16th of Thermidor by a member of
the section of Gravilliers who was with the invading
troops and was an eyewitness (*Moniteur*, XXI, 385.
Quoted by Aulard, *Études et leçons*, Paris, 1893,
285). The same witness states that as the troops entered the city hall "a citizen who marched by the
side of Léonard Bourdon [the leader] fell under
the body of the younger Robespierre who had
thrown himself from a window." In other words, before the elder Robespierre shot himself, his brother
had sought to escape by jumping from the window.

The employees in the record office of the city hall
published an account of Robespierre's end in the
Journal de Perlet of the 24th of Thermidor (Aulard,
Études et leçons, Paris, 1893, 285). It describes first
the reading of the decree of the convention outlaw-
ing Robespierre and his associates. The document

was read and commented on by the mayor. "Then followed a period of silence broken by a pistol-shot in the passage-way between the hall of the council and that of the general assembly. The mayor left his seat and ran to the place from which the shot seemed to come. He came back at once, pale and trembling, and on all sides the cry was heard, 'Robespierre has blown out his brains!'"

The concierge, Michel Brochard, stated (Aulard, *Études et leçons,* Paris, 1893, 286): "The elder Robespierre shot himself with a pistol, the ball of which, missing him, came within three inches of hitting me. I came near being killed by it, as Robespierre fell upon me on leaving the hall of Égalité by the passage."

According to Léonard Gallois, a contemporary who gathered the oral tradition (Aulard, *Études et leçons,* Paris, 1893, 287), "the opinion of all the old friends of Robespierre, of his sisters and of his contemporaries is that he shot himself with a pistol and broke his jaw. The wound proves convincingly that he put the muzzle of the pistol into his mouth."

Barère, in his report to the convention on the morning of the 10th of Thermidor said "Robespierre shot himself" (Aulard, *Études et leçons,* Paris, 1893, 287). Dulac, an employee of the Committee of Public Safety, testified a year later (Aulard, *Études et leçons,* Paris, 1893, 286): "I found him [Robespierre] stretched out near a table, suffering

from a pistol wound, the ball having entered an inch
and a half below the lower lip and passed out below
the left cheek-bone."

Finally, we have the report of the surgeons who
examined the wound at five o'clock on the morning
of the 10th of Thermidor (*Histoire parlementaire,*
XXXIV, 90) : "We noticed first of all," runs the
record, "that the entire face was swollen, more pronounced on the left; there was also an erosion of the
skin and ecchymosis of the eye on the same side. The
pistol had been discharged on a level with the mouth,
an inch from the commissure of the lips. As its direction [the direction of the ball] was oblique from outside in, from left to right, from above down, and as
the wound penetrated the mouth, it affected exter-
nally the skin, the cellular tissue, the triangular mus-
cles, *buccinateur,* etc. On introducing the finger into
the mouth, we found a fracture with splinters at the
angle of the lower jaw and we drew out two canine
teeth, a first molar and some pieces of bone from
this angle; but it was impossible for us to follow the
course of the bullet and we found no counter-opening
and no trace of the ball." The surgeons remark on
"the smallness of the wound."

Setting aside the inference that the bullet entered
from the outside and followed a downward course
from left to right,—for this is nothing but inference,
—would it be possible to imagine a report that could
give stronger support to the contemporary belief
that Robespierre had shot himself by placing the

muzzle of a pistol in his mouth? Could the state of things described by the surgeons be produced in any other way? If a pistol, held in the right hand, were discharged into the mouth would it not have broken the jaw bone on the left side, knocked out teeth, caused a swelling of the left side of the face, and could not the bullet have passed out through the cheek, making a small hole? Discard the assertion of Méda and all the evidence falls into place, even including the statement of the concierge that the bullet from Robespierre's pistol narrowly missed him.

And why should Robespierre not have tried to take his life? He had been outlawed; he had begun to sign his name to an insurrectionary and illegal document (see the facsimile of the original in the *Mémoires de Barras,* 4 vols., Paris, 1895, I, opposite page 194); the militia that had gathered in the square before the city hall had dispersed, the building was surrounded and being invaded by the troops of the convention. His friends were either trying to escape or committing suicide; if he did not take his own life, he would certainly be arrested and guillotined without trial. Why should he have hesitated?

All the evidence bearing on the event and the entire setting of it is of such a character that there is much ground for wonder that the statement of the gendarme Méda should ever have had any importance attached to it. He may have fired at Robespierre, he may have believed that he wounded him, but he certainly did not make the wound described by the surgeons, and there was no other. That Robespierre shot himself is highly probable.

If the problem of the attempted suicide of Robespierre were treated as the subject of a monograph instead of an episode in a history of the revolution, the matter relegated to a note in the general work might all be incorporated in the text. In either case, it is difficult to draw with precision the line between what should go into the text and what into the note. The rule is to state in the text the conclusions reached from a study of the evidence and to explain in the text how those results were reached. If now and then some of the proof slips into the text it need not be looked upon as an unpardonable offence against the canons of historical exposition.

The exposition of the results of historical research should always be supplemented by a critical bibliography and at times appendixes may be necessary. A critical bibliography should consist of a complete list of all the material, sources and secondary, used in the preparation of the history. The list of secondary works should not consist of all that has been written on the subject, but only such as still have scientific value. It should include articles in reviews as well as larger histories and monographs. The works should be arranged alphabetically, according to the authors' names. To give the bibliography a critical character, a note should be added to each title indicating the nature and value of the work. The titles should be given in full, with the name of author, including initials, the title of the work, number of volumes, edition, place and date of publication. All of these details are indispensable.

The sources should be presented apart from the secondary works and divided into groups containing the printed and the manuscript material. In each group, the matter should be arranged systematically and alphabetically so that any material looked for may be found easily. The printed sources can be naturally arranged under such heads as "Official Documents," "Correspondence," "Newspapers," "*Mémoires*," etc., and under these subdivisions, alphabetically according to authors, titles of newspapers, collections of documents, etc. In the division devoted to manuscript sources, the usual practice is to arrange the material according to the archives, and under the archives according to the title of the document. The full title of each document and the exact indication of where it is found in the archives should be given.

With each group of material should go a critical note indicating what the material is and what its value is. The purpose of these critical notes, whether given in the body of the work, in the bibliography or in an appendix, is to acquaint the student with the results of the historian's critical investigations. For example, some sources, hitherto anonymous, undated, or considered independent have been localized. There is no place in the text for the proof of

the work and yet it is quite as important that it
should be made public and preserved as that the
facts should be narrated. If the matter is brief, some
of it may go into notes in the body of the book; much
of it may be included in the bibliograhy; sometimes,
if the study is a long one, it may be relegated to an
appendix. This bibliographical work should be done
with great care that it may be utilized readily and
confidently.

The appendix is the place for unpublished sources,
if it seems desirable to make them accessible to the
reader, for maps, diagrams, tables and long critical
studies dealing with such questions as genuineness,
authorship, time and place of writing and independence of sources. A source, published in an appendix,
should be reproduced in the original language, although not necessarily in the original orthography.
The practice today is to modernize capitalization,
spelling and punctuation, unless the text should happen to have some philological value, when, of course,
the original form should be retained. The source
should be accompanied with an indication of its provenance, critical notes on its value and any explana-
tions that may be helpful in utilizing it.

We have traversed the long and difficult road
from the choice of a subject to the editing of a document for an appendix; it is the road every student of
history must traverse who would know how the past
is restored from a critical study of the documents.
To become familiar, the road must be travelled

many times. Although the technique of historical method is not to be mastered for the mere purpose of mastering it, but that it may be used in the search for historical truth, yet, as in any other subject, the mastery of the technique is the indispensable condition of successful work. Naturally, what has been presented here is but an elementary sketch intended to serve only as an introduction to historical work, to help the student through his first attempt at research.

I have attempted to make clear the difference between the method of history and that of natural science, and to justify the claim that some knowledge of historical method should form a part of the training of every educated man and woman, while a considerable acquaintance with the method should be required of every teacher of history. I have sought to demonstrate the necessity of developing the historical consciousness by the teaching of history in the schools and of supplying a sound base for such instruction through scientific historical study. Finally, I have hoped to awaken in a few the laudable ambition to contribute something to the exact knowledge of man's past life in society through acquaintance with the methods of historical research and their conscious and careful application. If the book accomplishes one or more of these things, it will serve a good purpose.

BIBLIOGRAPHY

INTRODUCTION

A. WORKS ON HISTORICAL METHOD.

Bernheim, Ernst. *Lehrbuch der historischen Methode.* Sixth edition. Leipzig, 1908.

Freeman, E. A. *The Methods of Historical Study.* London, 1886.

Langlois, Ch. V. et Seignobos, Ch. *Introduction aux études historiques.* Paris, 1898. English translation by G. B. Berry (Holt & Co., 1898) now out of print.

Vincent, John Martin. *Historical Research.* New York, 1911.

Bernheim's volume is the standard textbook on historical method, having no rival in any language. It deals with all phases of method from the definition of history to the philosophy of history. Each chapter is accompanied by a detailed bibliography embracing everything of importance that has been published on the topic. For the advanced student, nothing can take the place of Bernheim. It is not a work to be read once and laid aside, but an encyclopedia of method to be kept on the work table.

It is unnecessary to enumerate all the introductions to historical method that have been published. Of the works that have appeared in English, Freeman's volume is unsystematic and incomplete. It is interesting because of the element of personal experience it contains, but should not be recommended to beginners as a guide. The work of

Langlois and Seignobos and that of Vincent were intended to serve that purpose. The first volume was the outcome of a series of lectures delivered to beginning students at the Sorbonne; Professor Vincent's attractive volume, intended "for the advanced student who is about to enter the field of research, either as a profession or as a serious avocation," stresses mediaeval history and will be helpful as an introduction to students intending to specialize in that field.

B. Works on the Logic of History.

Adler, Max. *Kausalität und Teleologie im Streite um die Wissenschaft.* Wien, 1904.

Croce, Benedetto. *Il concetto della storia nelle sue relazioni col concetto dell' arte.* Second edition, Roma, 1896.

Droysen, J. G. *Principles of History.* Translated by E. B. Andrews. Boston, 1893.

Fling, F. M. "Historical Synthesis," *American Historical Review,* Vol. ix, No. 1, October, 1903.

Gottl, F. *Die Grenzen der Geschichte.* Leipzig, 1904.

Hobhouse, L. T. *Development and Purpose.* London, 1913.

Hughes, Percy. "The Concept Action in History and in the Natural Sciences," *Columbia University Contributions to Philosophy, Psychology, and Education,* Vol. x, No. 3.

Kistiakowski, Th. *Gesellschaft und Einzelwesen.* Berlin, 1899.

Lacombe, P. *De l'histoire considérée comme science.* Paris, 1894.

Lamprecht, Karl. *Die kulturhistorische Methode.* Berlin, 1900.

BIBLIOGRAPHY

Lask, Emil. *Fichte's Idealismus und die Geschichte.* Leipzig, 1902.

Medicus, Fritz. "Kant und Ranke," *Kantstudien,* Band viii, Heft 2-3, Berlin, 1903.

Münsterberg, H. *Psychology and Life* (1899), chapter v, "Psychology and History."

Münsterberg, H. *Philosophie der Werthe.* Leipzig, 1908.

Naville, Adrien. *Nouvelle classification des sciences.* Second edition. Paris, 1901.

Rickert, Heinrich. *Die Grenzen der naturwissenschaftlichen Begriffsbildung.* Leipzig, 1902. Second edition, 1913.

Robinson, J. H. *The New History.* New York, 1912.

Show, A. B. "The New Culture-History in Germany," *The History Teacher's Magazine,* October, 1913.

Windelband, Wilhelm. *Geschichte und Naturwissenschaft.* Strassburg, 1900.

Xenopol, A. D. *Les principes fondamentaux de l'histoire.* Paris, 1899.

Xenopol, A. D. "Natur und Geschichte," *Historische Zeitschrift,* 113 Band, 1 Heft.

The list of titles given above does not constitute an exhaustive bibliography of the growing literature on the logic of history. It is, however, representative and will enable the student to get fully oriented on the subject.

Naville's little volume may serve as an introduction, giving the position of history among the sciences as a whole. My article on "Historical Synthesis" traces briefly the history of the debate between history and natural science from Buckle to the present time. The attempt to make a natural science of history has failed.

The theory of Lamprecht, the last protagonist of the application of the method of natural science to history, is presented in his *Kulturhistorische Methode;* a criticism of the theory will be found in the article by Professor Show.

Windelband's address on *Geschichte und Naturwissenschaft* is an excellent summary of the logic of history as distinguished from that of natural science. The great work on the logic of history is Rickert's *Grenzen.* For the specialist in history it should be a companion volume to Bernheim's *Lehrbuch* and should be worked over as carefully.

Droysen's *Principles* may be read with profit after Rickert has cleared the way. The forerunner of Windelband and Rickert was Fichte, and Lask's study makes clear how important a part he had in the evolution of the logic of history, "the logic of the irrational."

Besides Lamprecht, Lacombe may serve as a type of the sociologist who cannot understand that the end aimed at determines the method to be employed; he, too, would "raise history to the rank of a science" by making it something other than history. Professor Robinson's studies on "The New History" should be read in connection with Lamprecht's volume; he too believes that the historian should learn from the natural scientist and takes no notice of the logical difference between a synthesis formulating laws and one presenting a complex, unique whole. All the sociologists do not belong to the group that assumes that the only way to render history scientific is to transform it into a natural science. Simmel and Kistiakowski accept the logical distinction between history and natural science.

Among writers on the logic of history, difference of opinion exists touching the underlying principles of historical synthesis. Münsterberg emphasizes content as opposed to form and insists that the characteristic content of history is "individual will-acts" and "that the endless world of will-acts forms the only material of history": his *Philosophie der Werthe* distinguishes the "values" lying at the base of historical construction from those supplying the *apriori* of the natural sciences.

Hughes points out that history deals with "action" as opposed to "law" in the natural sciences and seeks to demonstrate that the word "action" will do for the logic of historical science all that is done by the term "individual" and will, at the same time, give a content to history.

Adler, while accepting the distinction between history and science, attempts to demonstrate that natural science alone can be called science, as it searches for "laws." The answer is, of course, that if science is organized knowledge, history has as good a right to the use of the term as botany or chemistry. This debate on the right of the natural sciences to monopolize the term science is a survival of the period in which it was believed there was no science but natural science.

Gottl tries to make clear the distinction between history, on the one side, and geology, geography and anthropology on the other. The last three form a group to which Gottl gives the name "metahistorik": geology treats an occurrence as a series of appearances due to natural laws and intelligible through analogy; history, on the other hand, from the ground of logical thought, conceives of the occurrence as a complex of rational activities and understands it from its own inner relations and connections.

Medicus sets over against *substance* and *causality*—the categories of natural science—*potentiality* and *teleology* as the categories of historical science.

Xenopol opposes "historical series," dealing with "successive facts," to "natural laws," dealing with "facts of repetition."

Hobhouse distinguishes between "mechanism" and "teleology" and asserts that "to explain a thing may be to refer it (teleologically) to its place in a system which as a whole has value, or (mechanically) to its immediate antecedent in indifference to any system. The full explanation of a machine involves both kinds of explanation." This volume is the most recent contribution to the literature of revolt against the claim of natural science to supply an exhaustive method for discovering the truth of reality. The question of the justification of historical method is not a matter which concerns the scientist alone; it is of universal human importance.

CHAPTER II

CHOICE OF A SUBJECT. COLLECTION AND CLASSIFICATION OF MATERIAL

A. CHOICE OF A SUBJECT.

Helpful articles, suggesting subjects for investigation.
1. *The American Historical Review:* J. W. Thompson, "Profitable Fields of Investigation in Mediaeval History" (xviii, No. 3); J. H. Robinson, "The Study of the Lutheran Revolt" (viii, No. 2); J. H. Robinson, "Recent Tendencies in the Study of the French Revolution" (xi, No. 3); W. E. Lingelbach, "Historical Investigation and the Commercial History of the Napoleonic Era" (xix, No. 2); A. L. Cross, "Legal Materials as Sources for the Study of Modern English History" (xix, No. 4); G. S. Callender, "The Position of American Economic History" (xix, No. 1); A. E. Stone, "Some Problems of Southern Economic History" (xiii, No. 4).

BIBLIOGRAPHY

2. Proceedings of the American Historical Association: S. B. Fay, "Materials for the Study of Germany in the Sixteenth and Seventeenth Centuries" (1911, pages 79-87).

3. *Revue de synthèse historique:* Many valuable articles on various periods and countries, showing what work has been done and what remains to be done.

B. BIBLIOGRAPHY.

The best introduction to bibliographical work is Langlois, Ch. V. *Manuel de bibliographie historique* (Paris, 1904). The great publication of the annual historical output is the *Jahresberichte der Geschichtwissenschaften,* published at Berlin.

For the French revolution, indispensable volumes are: Caron, P. *Manuel pratique pour l'étude de la révolution française* (Paris, 1912); Tuetey, A. *Les papiers des assemblées de la révolution aux archives nationales* (Paris, 1908); Schmidt, C. *Les sources de l'histoire de France depuis 1789 aux archives nationales* (Paris, 1907); the annual *Répertoire* of historical works published by the *Revue d'histoire moderne.*

The bibliographies of the different periods and countries will be found in Bernheim.

Some helpful articles in the *American Historical Review* are: G. L. Burr, "European Archives" (vii, No. 4); C. M. Andrews, "Material in British Archives for American Colonial History" (x, No. 2); J. F. Jameson, "Gaps in the Published Records of United States History" (xi, No. 4); P. Mantoux, "French Reports of British Parliamentary Debates in the Eighteenth Century" (xii, No. 2); H. E. Bolton, "Material for Southwestern History in the Central Archives of Mexico" (xiii, No. 3).

CHAPTER III
CRITICISM OF THE SOURCES

A. FORGERIES.

Journal of a Spy in Paris during the Reign of Terror, January-July, 1794, by Raoul Hesdin. London, John Murray, 1895.

My article on the third volume of the *Mémoires* of Bailly is found in *La révolution française* (November 14, 1902), "Une pièce fabriquée; le troisième volume des mémoires de Bailly."

Maxime de la Rocheterie et le Marquis de Beaucourt. *Lettres de Marie Antoinette.* 2 vols. Paris, 1895.

Otto Becker. *Die Verfassungspolitik der französischen Regierung beim Beginn der grossen Revolution.* Berlin, 1910.

On the genuineness of the *Mémoires de Talleyrand* see the *Revue historique,* xlviii, 2, article by Alfred Stern, xlix, 1, article by Flammermont and the *Historische Zeitschrift,* Band LXVIII, 58, article by Paul Bailleu.

A recent publication by O. G. de Heidenstam of a volume on *Marie Antoinette, Fersen et Barnave, leur correspondance* (Paris, 1913), is considered a forgery by Glagau (*Annales revolutionnaires,* mai-juin, 1914), but probably all the errors cited by Glagau can be explained on the ground of careless and unscientific editing.

B. LOCALIZATION.

Articles in the *American Historical Review* on localization and evaluation of the sources are: S. B. Platner, "The Credibility of Early Roman History" (vii, No. 2); F. M.

BIBLIOGRAPHY

Fling, "The Authorship of the Journal d'Adrien Duques-noy" (viii, No. 1); D. C. Munro, "The Speech of Pope Urban II at Clermont, 1095" (xi, No. 2); R. C. H. Catterall, "The Credibility of Marat" (xvi, No. 1); Carl Becker, "Horace Walpole's Memoirs of the Reign of George III" (xvi, No. 2); E. G. Bourne, "The Authorship of the Federalist" (ii, Nos. 3, 4).

My studies of the *Mémoires de Bailly* will be found in the *University Studies* of the University of Nebraska, iii, No. 4.

The letters of Capello, Desmoulins and Stael-Holstein are translated in my *Source Studies on the French Revolution: The Royal Session.* Lincoln, 1907.

Arthur Young's Travels in France edited by Miss Betham-Edwards. London, 1892.

Kovalevsky, Massimo. *I dispacci degli ambasciatori veneti alla corte di Francis durante la revoluzione.* Torino, 1895.

De Kermaingant P.-L. *Souvenirs et fragments pour servir aux mémoires de ma vie et de mon temps par le Marquis de Bouillé.* 3 vols. Paris, 1906-1911. See reviews in *American Historical Review,* XII, 924, XV, 413, XVII, 372.

For the question of the *Moniteur, Journal des débats* and the *Histoire . . . par deux amis de la liberte,* see Carl Christophelsmeier, "The Fourth of August, 1789," in the *University Studies* of the University of Nebraska, vi, No. 4.

Dubois-Crancé. *Analyse de la révolution française.* Paris, 1885.

Thibaudeau. *Mes souvenirs,* published with an introduction by Th. Ducrocq, with no indication of place or date of publication, but published after 1895.

[193]

We have positive proof that the heads of the guards were in Paris before the king and queen left Paris. See the study on "The Insurrection of October 5 and 6, 1789" in my *Source Problems on the French Revolution* (Harper & Brothers), pp. 234, 246.

On "The Oath of the Tennis Court," see the study in the collection of sources mentioned above, *Source Problems on the French Revolution.*

On the tricolored cockade, the sources cited are: *Procès-verbal . . . des électeurs de Paris* (3 vols. Paris, 1790), ii, 92; *Oeuvres de Camille Desmoulins* (3 vols. Paris, 1886), ii, 97; Gouverneur Morris, *Diary and Letters* (2 vols. New York, 1888), i, 131; Duquesnoy, *Journal* (2 vols. Paris, 1894), i, 408; Grouchy et Guillois, *La révolution française. Correspondance du Bailli de Virieu* (Paris, (n.d.)), p. 121.

On Mirabeau's speech of June 23, 1789, see my study in *Source Problems on the French Revolution*, "The Royal Session on June 23, 1789."

CHAPTER VII

SYNTHESIS, OR GROUPING OF THE FACTS

On values in history see:

  Grotenfeld, A. *Die Wertschätzung in der Geschichte.* Leipzig, 1903.

  Grotenfeld, A. *Geschichtliche Wertmasstäbe in der Geschichtsphilosophie.* Leipzig, 1905.

  Rickert. *Die Grenzen,* etc. (first edition), 371.

  Rickert. *Geschichtsphilosophie* (1905).

On the meaning of history see:

BIBLIOGRAPHY

Bergson, H. *L'évolution créatrice*. Sixth edition. Paris, 1910.

Eucken, R. *Der Kampf um einen geistigen Lebensinhalt.* Leipzig, 1896.

Medicus (already cited).

On causality see:

Rickert. *Die Grenzen,* 392.

Xenopol, A. "La causalité dans la série historique," in the *Revue de synthèse historique,* xxvii, 3.

On historical series, besides the article of Xenopol above cited, see his volume on *Les principes fondamentaux de l'histoire.*

PRINTED IN THE UNITED STATES OF AMERICA

DATE DUE